The Government/Press Connection

Newswork 2

The Government/Press Connection

Press Officers and Their Offices

STEPHEN HESS

THE BROOKINGS INSTITUTION
Washington, D.C.

Library of Congress Cataloging in Publication data:

Hess, Stephen.
  The government/press connection.

  At head of title: Newswork.
  Bibliography: p.
  Includes index.
  1. Government publicity—United States.
2. Government and the press—United States. I. Title.
JK849.A3H47 1984   353.0081'9   84-17014
ISBN 0-8157-3596-0
ISBN 0-8157-3595-2 (pbk.)

1 2 3 4 5 6 7 8 9

THE BROOKINGS INSTITUTION is an independent organization devoted to nonpartisan research, education, and publication in economics, government, foreign policy, and the social sciences generally. Its principal purposes are to aid in the development of sound public policies and to promote public understanding of issues of national importance.

The Institution was founded on December 8, 1927, to merge the activities of the Institute for Government Research, founded in 1916, the Institute of Economics, founded in 1922, and the Robert Brookings Graduate School of Economics and Government, founded in 1924.

The Board of Trustees is responsible for the general administration of the Institution, while the immediate direction of the policies, program, and staff is vested in the President, assisted by an advisory committee of the officers and staff. The by-laws of the Institution state: "It is the function of the Trustees to make possible the conduct of scientific research, and publication, under the most favorable conditions, and to safeguard the independence of the research staff in the pursuit of their studies and in the publication of the results of such studies. It is not a part of their function to determine, control, or influence the conduct of particular investigations or the conclusions reached."

The President bears final responsibility for the decision to publish a manuscript as a Brookings book. In reaching his judgment on the competence, accuracy, and objectivity of each study, the President is advised by the director of the appropriate research program and weighs the views of a panel of expert outside readers who report to him in confidence on the quality of the work. Publication of a work signifies that it is deemed a competent treatment worthy of public consideration but does not imply endorsement of conclusions or recommendations.

The Institution maintains its position of neutrality on issues of public policy in order to safeguard the intellectual freedom of the staff. Hence interpretations or conclusions in Brookings publications should be understood to be solely those of the authors and should not be attributed to the Institution, to its trustees, officers, or other staff members, or to the organizations that support its research.

Foreword

IN A previous study (*The Washington Reporters*, Brookings Institution, 1981) Stephen Hess, a senior fellow in the Brookings Governmental Studies program, provided a perspective on the journalists who cover the U.S. government for the American commercial news media. In this new volume he turns his attention to the personnel and operations of government press offices. The study is based on a year Hess spent as an observer at the White House, State Department, Department of Defense, Department of Transportation, and Food and Drug Administration.

The Government/Press Connection can be appreciated on a number of levels: as a public administration study of a government function that has received scant attention from scholars; as a new interpretation of the utility of leaks for intragovernmental communication; and as a series of shrewd insights into common occurrences and practices that we tend to take for granted, including government briefings, handouts, and even the press clippings that circulate in a government agency. Readers will probably be most interested, however, in the evaluation of the degree to which government press operations may or may not manipulate public opinion. Hess differs with the conventional wisdom. He finds little evidence that press offices are propaganda machines distorting the nation's public dialogue. Others, of course, may draw different conclusions from the material he presents.

For the opportunity to have been an inside observer, the author wishes to thank David R. Gergen and Larry M. Speakes, White House; Dean E. Fischer and Alan Romberg, State Department; Henry E. Catto, Jr., Department of Defense; Linda J. Gosden, Department of Transportation; and Wayne L. Pines, Food and Drug Administration.

The author's research was supported by grants from the John M. Olin Foundation, the Earhart Foundation, and the National Press Foundation. He is grateful to Michael S. Joyce, Richard A. Ware, Joseph R. Slevin, Frank A. Aukofer, and Don Larrabee for the special interest they have taken in his work.

vii

Thoughtful critiques of draft chapters were made by Martha Derthick, Jerry W. Friedheim, Herbert Kaufman, Morton Lebow, Robert J. McCloskey, Don Oberdorfer, Paul E. Peterson, A. James Reichley, Margaret M. Rhoades, Kate Semerad, and Leon V. Sigal.

The author appreciates the creative editorial services of James R. Schneider, the administrative support of Diane Hodges, and the secretarial assistance of Pamela Harris. The book was proofread by Donna Carter and the index was prepared by Florence Robinson.

All the views expressed in this book are those of the author and should not be ascribed to the John M. Olin Foundation, the Earhart Foundation, the National Press Foundation, or the trustees, officers, or other staff members of the Brookings Institution.

BRUCE K. MACLAURY
President

July 1984
Washington, D.C.

For Beth

Author's Note

THE OBSERVATIONS in this study are primarily based on an outsider's year inside the press offices of five federal agencies in Washington, first at the Food and Drug Administration, then at the Pentagon, the Department of Transportation, the State Department, and the White House. I spent from one month to three months at each place.

Starting in September, 1981, my days were devoted to following press officers as they went about their business. I listened to them talk on the phone, asked them to explain the calls they were making or receiving, attended their staff meetings, and accompanied them to press conferences, briefings, hearings, and to lunch. I read the contents of their "in" boxes and office files. When there were pressrooms at the agencies, I observed and interviewed the reporters, attempting to see the press officers through their eyes. I also talked with other government officials about them.

The technique of site observation has an honorable tradition in the social sciences, particularly in cultural anthropology, and as my colleague Herbert Kaufman points out, "The benefits of this mode of research have recently been winning renewed favor among students of organizations."[1] Moreover, it has been successfully used by two creative students of news processing, Edward Jay Epstein and Herbert J. Gans, who were allowed inside news organizations.[2] Still, when I began this project I wondered whether disseminating news, the work of press offices, was too sensitive in political terms to be studied effectively in this way. Would press officers, for example, discuss among themselves what not to tell reporters when there was an outsider present? In some cases permission to be an observer may have been granted to me because of prior personal or political contacts—I served on White House staffs in 1958–61 and in 1969. But after this initial foot in the door, I found that workers seemed to go about their business and to speak freely, probably because I hung around long enough and conducted myself in a nonthreatening manner. In short, the technique seemed valid.

To the best of my knowledge, the only meetings I was excluded from were supervisors' evaluations of the merits of particular workers. At several agencies I was required to get security clearances, which may have contributed to my bona fides: in a sense the government had officially certified me as trustworthy. Indeed, as I was to discover at times, one of my tougher tasks was to keep from being drawn into the activities I was there to observe. An observer does not advise, even when advice is solicited. I was also lucky. It was obviously mandatory that I not carry messages back and forth between officials and reporters, and my luck was that there were no leaks I could have been blamed for.

Generally I took notes only in meetings in which everyone was taking notes or in interviews where it was clearly expected of me. But each night, with the day's impressions fresh in mind, I wrote a log of what I had seen and heard and what I thought it all meant. When my entries became repetitious, I concluded I had probably absorbed all that I was capable of and that it was time to move to another agency.

I made no commitments to limit what I would write about other than a promise to show the draft manuscript to key officials who could then try to convince me of my mistakes. I offered no confidentiality, and only one person requested that our conversations be put on background, meaning that I could use his statements only if they were not attributed to him. Where I have not identified participants by name it is because I preferred to describe them by what they did or because I felt I had gathered information by eavesdropping on people with whom I had not established ground rules.

Because most of the executive branch information that relates to America's place in the world is funneled through the White House and the Departments of State and Defense, three agencies that I elsewhere call "the golden triangle,"[3] I naturally chose to observe their press offices. But I also wanted to go to agencies whose activities are seldom reported on front pages or by television networks unless there is something like a ban on saccharin or an air controller's strike. As parts of this outer ring of government, the Food and Drug Administration and the Department of Transportation were repeatedly recommended to me by reporters and officials for having good press operations. These choices were felicitous because I found that when people are proud of their skills, they are most willing to have a stranger look over their shoulders. I did not seek out agencies with a reputation for inefficiency or a history of scandal: the purpose of my study was to learn about a special type of government function, not to award performance ratings in a sort of Michelin guide to Washington press offices. Then too, I sought observation points at different levels of government. The view at the Department of Transportation was from a cabinet member's perspective; the view at the Food and Drug Administration was through the other end of the telescope in that the agency is three managerial layers and twenty miles removed from the Office of the Secretary of Health and Human Services.

In some ways my observations were necessarily limited. A year spent wandering around government press offices does not allow an observer to compare the styles of successive administrations—and as Rush Taylor, director of news operations at the State Department, pointed out to me, "the differences in press relations from one administration to another can be staggering."* Nor can one year enable observations of changes caused by the length of time an administration has been in office: first years and fourth years have very different looks, as Michael Grossman and Martha Kumar suggest in their cyclical theory of relations between reporters and presidents.[4] On the other hand, the timing of this project did ease my access to press offices and probably was conducive to the candor of press officers: the project came early enough in the life of the Reagan administration that the president and his appointees still held relatively benign attitudes toward outsiders.

My observations were also probably influenced by common variables that affect government relations with reporters. The season of the year makes a difference; for instance, January—just before the president sends the budget to Congress—is the leakiest month in Washington, and tension between the government and the press can be expected to increase. Not surprisingly, it was in January 1982 that the White House tried to crack down on officials' contacts with the press and in January 1983 that President Reagan complained he had "had it up to [his] keister with these leaks."[5] Personalities also make a difference. A veteran Pentagon reporter described Caspar Weinberger as a "mouthy secretary" who talked so frequently on the record that he had become a "drug on the market." To prove the point, he held up a morning newspaper in which the defense chief's appearance on a Sunday television program was only the third lead. Across the Potomac in Foggy Bottom a veteran diplomatic reporter talked about Alexander Haig as a secretary of state whose contempt for the press was so palpable that he had not even bothered to master the difference between "off the record" and "on back-ground."[6] Reporters further contend that the relative merits of press secretaries make a difference. Television network correspondent Barrie Dunsmore fondly remembered Secretary of State Cyrus Vance's spokesman, Hodding Carter:

* All persons are identified by the title they had at the time I interviewed or observed them.

"Sometimes you called him with a little question and you got a big answer."

To arrive at generalizations, therefore, I have tested my observations through interviews with reporters and civil servants whose experiences span more than one presidency and interviews with press spokesmen from previous administrations. The study reflects comments from press officers under five secretaries of state and five secretaries of defense. Of course, memories will play wondrous tricks, and some participants will feel the need to defend and perhaps retrospectively correct the historical record. But I hope that this mix of past experiences and present observations will provide a basis of valid impressions that other researchers will be able to confirm by more systematic means.

S.H.

Contents

1. Carping Journalists and Incompetent Press Officers   1
2. The Organization of Press Offices   7
3. Press Secretaries and Career Press Officers   18
4. Routine Activities   38
5. Reactions to Crises   54
6. Briefings   61
7. Leaks and Other Informal Communications   75
8. Reporter Status and Government Media Strategies   95
9. Reflections on Government/Press Relations   107
   Documents   116
   Notes   140
   Index   154

CHAPTER 1

Carping Journalists and Incompetent Press Officers

THE DEVELOPMENT of government press offices is a twentieth-century phenomenon, dating back to Woodrow Wilson's creation of the Committee on
Public Information during World War I. The committee was a sort of
ministry of propaganda whose news division churned out an average of more
than ten releases a day.

Before the turn of the century there was little need for formal links between
journalists and officials. After all, in 1888, when there were 38 states in the
union and 330 members of the House of Representatives, the *Congressional
Directory* shows that the entire official Washington press corps consisted of
127 reporters. Even the White House was not a regular beat until 1896 when
William Price, a reporter for the *Washington Star*, stationed himself outside
the building to interview Grover Cleveland's visitors. Price's initiative inspired
imitators. On a winter day in 1902, Theodore Roosevelt saw reporters huddled
around the north portico and invited them inside. Later that year he had a
pressroom built in the new west wing which, George Juergens notes in his
history of the relationship between president and press during the Progressive
Era, "conferred a sort of legitimacy on their presence. . . . They were no
longer there just as guests of the president."[1]

Wilson was the first chief executive to hold regular press conferences,
starting when 125 reporters crowded into the East Room on a Saturday
afternoon in March 1913. And although Herbert Hoover would be the first
president to have an assistant with the title of press secretary, Joseph Tumulty
of Wilson's staff performed this role, briefing about 30 reporters from the
major news organizations each morning at ten.

Pressroom, press conference, press secretary, press office, press release:

the development of government mechanisms to service the news media was a product of mutual advantage, not a constitutional responsibility of the Republic. Activist presidents and expansionist newspapers occurred at the same time and needed each other.[2] With a new vision of America's significance in the world, Teddy Roosevelt flexed the nation's muscles, sending the fleet around the world, dispatching the Marines to the Dominican Republic, and digging the Panama Canal. Washington was becoming exciting news. And The Hero of San Juan Hill, the trustbuster, the activist president personified, also wanted to be news, and was. Certainly never before, and debatably never since, has there been a president so made for headline writers and political cartoonists. "He really believes he is the American flag," said author John Jay Chapman.[3]

Meanwhile publishers, the Joseph Pulitzers and William Randolph Hearsts, were becoming the impressarios of a technology that featured Linotype and high-speed presses. The speed and printing capability enabled them to reach a truly mass market, one that advertisers paid handsomely to court. Newspaper readership doubled in the last two decades of the nineteenth century and almost tripled by the time Roosevelt left his "bully pulpit" in 1909.[4]

The story from Washington became infinitely more complicated and even more important after the whirlwind that was Franklin Roosevelt and his New Deal. As Leo C. Rosten wrote in his study of Washington reporters in the 1930s, "Within a few weeks after Mr. Roosevelt took office . . . [reporters] discovered that they were expected to write about the gold standard and the devaluation of the dollar, the reconstruction of industrial relations under NRA, a farm program, collective bargaining, public works, relief measures, national resources, and national planning. . . . The American public began to devour a *kind* of news with which most newspapermen had not been trained to cope."[5] The press corps grew because government grew. Government press operations grew because the press corps grew. Both grew because of increased complexities. Government took on more complicated questions that needed more explanation.[6] Government workers were increasingly technologists, and their work and speech needed to be translated for journalists.[7] At the same time, the news media became more technologically complicated, which meant that government officials would have to understand their special needs and limitations. Thus specialized government press officers were added both to service the media and to explain them to other government workers.

By 1980 the U.S. Office of Personnel Management reported that there were 2,900 federal public information specialists (GS-1081), another 2,178 writer-editors (GS-1082), and others who performed information functions regardless of their job descriptions.[8] These numbers, however, hardly justify claims that government is spending "at least $1 billion a year to inform and sell the American people" or "at least 2.5 billion dollars annually."[9] Such estimates are inflated; they include all advertising (military recruiting, stamp collecting, train riding), filmmaking, publications, and sometimes even the costs of the armed forces bands and precision flying units like the Blue Angels.[10] The subjects of this study—press offices—are actually very small operations by government standards. The State Department in Washington, for example, had 42 full-time public affairs advisers as of March 30, 1982. The Food and Drug Administration employs over 7,600 people, 9 of whom are press officers. Very few government buildings have pressrooms, and most government press officers have duties in addition to servicing reporters.

AS GOVERNMENT grows more important in our lives, the press also becomes more important. It is the vehicle through which we learn about government, so much so that Harvard political scientist Gary R. Orren suggests, "Will Rogers' famous quip about only knowing what he read in the papers seems to have been more prophetic than satirical." The quality and quantity of what government chooses to say about what it is doing are hardly inconsequential in a democracy. Intuitively, then, we think there is something very important about the relationship between government and the press, although, in fact, we know very little about this connection.

What has often been asserted about that connection over the past two decades is disturbing and adds urgency to our need to know more. "The government—the elected officials, the appointed executives, the various bureaucracies and bureaucrats—puts out only the information it wants to put out," says a report of the American Civil Liberties Union. "Through its vast network of public information offices, the government affirmatively broadcasts its side of the story, leaving out facts that might cloud the picture it wants to present. . . . Over the years, officials of the governments, particularly the federal government, have become as adept at playing this game as they are at drawing up yearly budgets. They play with a cynicism that suggests a good measure of contempt for the public."[11] Others write of government "flacks" who try to control the press, of government's "instinct" to manage and manipulate information, or of a "shadowy" government public relations machine that specializes in misinformation.[12] No wonder that Roger Rosenblatt of *Time* writes of "yet another smooth-voiced press officer," meaning not some special individual with a name, but rather an image akin to the nineteenth-century seller of snake oil.[13] Indeed, it is hard to find a discussion of modern government's relations with the press that does not include the words *manage, manipulate,* and *control.*

Yet there is a certain paradox to this emphasis on manipulation because another comment often made about government press officers is that they are not very good at their jobs. The *National Journal's* Dom Bonafede even found a government information specialist who said that federal public affairs officials are "pretty poor in general,"[14] and a newspaper article about a conscientious press officer describes her as atypical.[15] Marianne Means, of Hearst's Washington bureau, began a 1981 column, "President Reagan seems to be having trouble finding all that fraud and waste he promised to eliminate, so I've got a suggestion for him. He should wipe out all the so-called information specialists in the federal government. Nobody, including journalists, would miss them."[16]

The twin complaints seem to add up to an indictment of government press officers as incompetent manipulators.

But most of the comments about public information and its dispensers have one thing in common: they come from people who are or have been journalists. They also come from two schools of writing, Outrage and Anecdote. The former is primarily a product of the years spanning Vietnam and Watergate; the latter is represented by memoirs of various reporters who have covered Washington beats.[17] The first group of writers seems to start with the premise that government is corrupt or wrong (which is why it has so much to hide), while the other writers are more interested in telling amusing stories than in generalizing from their experiences. The outrage may be justified and the anecdotes may be accurate; we shall see. But journalists are hardly disinterested observers when the subject is government information policy and practices. Occasionally they have the good grace, as had William J. Small, to add: "I apologize to my friends in government for this book won't make them look good. I await their books to tell me all that's wrong with the press."[18] But except for former White House press secretaries, government information officers seldom write books from their perspective, and when they do, they mostly focus on crisis.[19]

The concept that "where you stand depends on where you sit"—known to public administrators as Miles's Law—is also germane to this controversy.[20] As a CBS correspondent, Edward R. Murrow narrated a television documentary that, when he became director of the U.S. Information Agency, he asked the British Broadcasting Corporation not to show.[21] Bill Moyers, when he was President Johnson's spokesman, said the press "generally tends to write its opinion of a matter and then seeks out facts for it." When he became a CBS correspondent, he narrated a TV documentary that President Reagan's spokesman said was "not fair" and "below the belt."[22]

Most writing about the government/press connection has also been limited in that scholars and journalists have overwhelmingly concentrated on the White House and election campaigns.[23] Those political scientists whose writings are most sensitive to the interplay between government and the news media have tended to be presidentialists.[24] In daily reportage from Washington, when there are stories about press relations, the emphasis is largely on the president: "This week, Reagan botched several questions at his news conference . . ." or "The television tube is this president's most potent weapon, as he proved again this week. . . ."[25]

What such exclusive focus means, of course, is that the remainder of the government/press connection is left underexplored. Indeed, the best volume on nonpresidential government press operations is a self-styled "guidebook for the practitioner,"[26] and the most frequently cited scholarly book on press relations in government agencies is a 1961 survey that interviewed thirty-eight public information officers and thirty-five newsmen.[27] Yet quantitatively, at least, most of the information that reaches the public through the news media comes from what Leon V. Sigal calls "routine channels." In his study on the organization and politics of newsmaking, Sigal analyzes 2,850 stories that had appeared in the *New York Times* and *Washington Post* and concludes that press officers or their routine news releases and briefings outnumber "enterprise channels" such as leaks by well over two to one.[28] Sigal looks at output—what appears in the press. In a previous study I looked at input—what reporters do to get their stories. We reached the same conclusions about the sources of news. Washington reporters covering national government, I found, contact press officers on almost half their stories.[29]

The press offices are what Don Oberdorfer of the *Washington Post* calls "the junction point where the government and the press meet." They are not the only junction points, of course.[30] But, Oberdorfer adds, "surely the guts of what passes across the news wires from Washington come from [press office] transactions. For most reporters, it's what it's all about—the clips, the releases, the briefings—and yet nobody ever studies that stuff."

This is the second volume in my Newswork series, which is based on the assumption that the press is a public policy institution and deserves the same kind of attention that has been paid to the presidency, judiciary, and legislature. The first book asked questions about the Washington reporters. Similar questions are now asked about the Washington press offices and officers: How do they organize their work and what are their relations within their organizations? Who are they? What do they do and how well do they do it? Although the methodologies of the *The Washington Reporters* (1981) and *The Government/Press Connection* are entirely different, they do suggest mirror images. One focuses on news gatherers, the other on information disseminators. Together, and with future studies, including one presently in the research stage on the Senate and the news media, they are meant to map the uncharted terrain where the press fits into the governmental process.

CHAPTER 2

The Organization
of Press Offices

IF AN ORGANIZATIONAL chart were being designed for a new government agency, it would probably include one box labeled *press* or *news media*. This unit would be responsible for all those duties that involve contacts with journalists—answering their inquiries, setting up interviews and briefings for them with the senior officials of the agency, writing news releases and fact sheets, and advising the agency head on press relations.

If this new agency is unimportant, the media's demands upon it may be so modest that responding to them is not a full-time job. The duties of the press office must therefore increase in order to keep the press officer gainfully employed. So the unit is renamed *communications* and takes on responsibility for the other ways that the agency tells the public about itself—writing speeches for senior agency officials, putting out agency publications, arranging for public service messages to be distributed to television and radio stations, and preparing audio-visual material for use in classrooms.

With these expanded duties there is now work for more than one person but not enough for two. A solution is to relabel the office *external relations* and to give it responsibility for all contacts between the agency and outside groups important to it—Congress, state and local governments, and consumers as well as the news media.

While this agency is hypothetical, each stage of growth experienced by its press office reflects the organization and duties of one or another actual press office. These offices are so small that they become likely candidates for incorporation into some larger entity, usually called *public affairs*. At the Pentagon, for example, there were fourteen press officers in 1981, eight in the Armed Forces News branch and six in the Defense News branch. They were part of what Assistant Secretary of Defense for Public Affairs Henry E. Catto, Jr., described as "the largest media conglomerate in the country":

7

Our Armed Forces Radio and TV consists of 34 TV stations, 95 radio stations, and 260 cable outlets. We publish two daily newspapers, a tabloid magazine, and a "thought" magazine, and we have one full-time RCA satellite—all of which are programmed to inform and entertain our troops abroad. We handle all freedom of information requests which come to the Pentagon. Our Community Relations Directorate is charged with seeing to it we are good citizens of the hundreds of communities where the armed forces live and operate throughout the country. We review all speeches given by the military for security and policy considerations. We operate a full-time journalism school which graduates 2,000 people a year. I accompany the Secretary on his overseas trips. Finally . . . we respond to the needs for information of reporters across the world, and, I, of course, brief the regular Pentagon correspondents twice a week.[1]

At the State Department, the press office—spokesman, deputy spokesman, director of news operations, and five press officers—is part of a public affairs bureau that produces publications and films, advises the secretary of state on American public opinion, arranges conferences and media engagements, and publishes *Foreign Relations of the United States*, a series of volumes that comprises the government's official diplomatic history.

The White House operation is somewhat different. In addition to the Office of the Press Secretary, which handles the chief executive's contacts with the news media, in 1969 President Nixon created a post for his old friend Herbert Klein, a San Diego newspaper editor. As director of communications, Klein was to coordinate the administration's press relations, as distinct from the president's. This office has been continued by Nixon's successors with minor permutations.[2] Such rearrangements sometimes have been used to solve sticky personnel problems: for example, the friction between David Gergen and Larry Speakes that developed after President Reagan's press secretary, James Brady, was shot in 1981.

These jobs involve only staff functions; press officers do not have line functions, that is, they do not run an agency's programs. Controversies over how to organize staff functions, including where to put the press office, keep recurring in the federal government. Part of the reason, I think, is that they are easy to fight over: by government standards they involve relatively few people, comparatively little money, and not many square feet of floor space. In addition, because the people who perform services for the powerful in government can be particularly adept at internal politicking, many of these reorganizations can be explained primarily in terms of game playing, the players with the most influence or cunning getting to expand their domains. In other instances staff people become infatuated with organization charts and the satisfactions that flow from moving the boxes around. In the short history of the Department of Transportation, as an illustration, the public affairs and congressional relations functions have been combined under Lyndon Johnson, separated under Richard Nixon, and separated, combined, and separated again under Jimmy Carter. Under some secretaries of state—William Rogers, Henry Kissinger, Edmund Muskie—the functions of the press spokesman have been separated from the other functions performed in the public affairs bureau; other secretaries of state—Cyrus Vance, Alexander Haig, George Shultz—have combined them. Regardless of organizational merit, all such rearrangements result in some short-term costs in staff morale and efficiency and relatively few reductions in expenditures.

The primary rationale for combining staff operations is usually "coordination" or "linkage." Related functions presumably benefit from being performed in close proximity, especially when an office is as small as Public Affairs at the Food and Drug Administration, where in 1981 most of the professional staff of its three entities (press, communications, and freedom of information) gathered weekly around a conference table.[3] But even at the FDA there were modest problems because the main press office was at headquarters in Rockville, Maryland, and a branch office was in downtown Washington near the Capitol. Linkages can fade rapidly as units grow or when they are not located in contiguous space, a situation that is often a by-product of growth.

When press relations, congressional relations, consumer relations, employee relations, intergovernmental relations, or various other staff functions are consolidated in a public affairs office, the element most important to a given agency or its head will soon consume the attention of the chief of public affairs, and the other duties will either be delegated to a deputy or left underattended. At the State Department, for instance, the assistant secretary for public affairs spends more than 80 percent of his time on responsibilities involving briefings and other press relations. At another agency I observed, the public affairs director spent more time on political affairs than on press relations. Thus consolidating responsibilities in the hands of one person usually means that secondary duties receive very little oversight, although increasing an administration's control over various offices staffed by career personnel may have been a paramount reason for initiating an agency's reorganization.

In the world of government perquisites, subtle differences that may affect the way an agency is organized stem from whether the official in charge of its press relations is an assistant secretary, spokesman, assistant secretary/

spokesman, press secretary, director, associate commissioner, or special assistant. The title of assistant secretary, which in the outer world suggests a junior clerk or a branch bank manager, is the only one of the above that in governmentese implies the jobholder was appointed by the president and confirmed by the Senate. Assistant secretary of defense for public affairs is a title that comes with the equivalent rank of a four-star general and rates a full colonel as a personal aide. However, not all assistant secretaryships are of equal importance. The State Department's assistant secretary for public affairs is one of the more lowly officers of that exalted rank, although its spokesman can have considerable clout, depending on the relationship to the secretary. This inequality suggests that a hidden agenda of some who have wished to combine the posts of assistant secretary and spokesman may have been to marry the protocol rank of the assistant secretary with the influence rank of the spokesman. Such a marriage might also raise the status of the nonpress functions of the public affairs bureau; that is, with an assistant secretary/spokesman the leverage of the spokesman would increase the resources of the assistant secretary's bureau.

On the other hand, the argument that upgrading the title of the press officer will improve an agency's relations with reporters is without merit. This ploy may work with political constituencies, hence the proliferation of special-interest representation in the White House, where various interest groups are thought to be flattered by having their own special assistant to the president.[4] But giving Ron Ziegler the title of special assistant rather than press secretary, as President Nixon initially did in 1969, had no effect on his relations with the White House press corps. Reporters do not care what the spokesman is called; that is a game bureaucrats play. Besides, in the news business the star reporter and the novice have the same title. Reporters show a similar lack of interest in the organizational structure of government press offices, despite the time they spend in them. I was constantly surprised that these professionally curious people had so little curiosity about press office budgets, personnel systems, or internal management. When reporters did not get what they wanted, they simply chalked it up to incompetence or laziness on the part of an individual press officer.

An argument for keeping the press secretary's function organizationally separate from other public affairs responsibilities is that most press chiefs are bad administrators. To look over the shoulder of an agency's press director in the days before word processors was often to see an executive tying up every typist in the office by compulsively reediting a draft document. Many press secretaries come to government from reporting jobs with news organizations or from public relations jobs in political campaigns, neither of which prepares them to be a manager. It almost seems as if the qualities necessary to be a good manager and those necessary to be a good spokesman are antithetical; at least they are seldom found in the same person. The point was forcefully presented to me at the Pentagon when reporters and staff chose to discuss the respective merits of Thomas Ross and Henry Catto, back-to-back assistant secretaries of defense for public affairs. Ross, who had been in the Washington bureau of the *Chicago Sun-Times*, was given high marks by reporters and low marks by staff; Catto, who had held a number of ambassadorial posts, was given lower marks by reporters and higher marks by staff.

An internal report on the public affairs functions of the State Department prepared by a four-person team of diplomats in 1979 when Hodding Carter III was both spokesman and assistant secretary concluded, "The Inspectors believe that, on the assumption that two very highly qualified individuals would be available, one as Spokesman of the Department and the other as Assistant Secretary of Public Affairs, and that both had good access to the Seventh Floor [Office of the Secretary of State], it would be preferable to handle these two functions separately. But the margin of advantage, while significant, is not overwhelming."[5] Generally, I agree. If the press function is important enough to an agency, it should be handled without the distraction of semirelated duties.[6]

AFTER OUR hypothetical agency has resolved where to put the press office box on its chart, it may turn to another organizational question: how much centralization is appropriate? Let us assume that the agency has acquired new programs and that each of these has required an administrative subunit. The agency now runs a museum, a zoo, and an arboretum, for example. Should each subunit have its own press office? If so, what should be the relationship between the zoo's press officer and the parent agency's press officer? Does the press officer at the zoo owe primary allegiance to the zoo's director? If so, what should be the relationship between the agency's press officer and the zoo's director?[7]

A decentralized organization raises some basic fears among those who come to Washington with a president-elect. Department press secretaries are generally political appointees or those who have otherwise proved their loyalty to the new administration. Subunit press officers, however, are generally career personnel whose political loyalties may lie elsewhere. Thus those charged with organizing press offices face the possibility that their publicity

apparatus is in the hands of a relatively autonomous enemy. Every administration since Franklin Roosevelt's has begun with the attitude that "it's us
against them," administration appointees against bureaucrats.

Actually, that attitude is mistaken. Politicians assume that civil service
employees have the same abiding interest in partisan politics that they have,
but this is rarely the case. Career personnel often have an abiding interest
in bureaucratic politics, the internal machinations of their agencies, which
may or may not work to the advantage of political appointees but not because
an administration is Republican or Democratic. The suspicious political
executive also fails to make a sufficient distinction between staff and line
operations. Press officers perform a services function, and as staff officers they
wish to develop special relationships with the supervisors on whom they must
depend for advancement. In effect, these relationships inform their concept
of loyalty. As the FDA press chief, a career employee, said of the FDA
commissioner, a political appointee, "the commissioner is the personification
of the agency. Most of my job is to get a good press for the commissioner."[8]

Each of the State Department's major geographic bureaus has a public
affairs adviser who spends most of his time working for the spokesman,
providing material that is needed for the noon briefings or composing answers
to questions that the spokesman has promised the reporters. Yet one of these
public affairs advisers reminded me that the assistant secretary in charge of
his bureau, not the spokesman, signed his efficiency report. While he liked
the spokesman and did not think himself disloyal, he left no doubt of from
whom he took orders and with whom he negotiated. At the same time, when
asked about the public affairs officers in places like the Bureau of Near
Eastern and South Asian Affairs or the Bureau of East Asian and Pacific
Affairs, Spokesman Dean Fischer replied, "they do not work for me, and,
obviously, I do not work for their bosses." Again, these comments have
nothing to do with being a career press officer or a political appointee;
indeed, the State Department is the rare government agency that sometimes
chooses career personnel to be spokesmen and often picks them to be the
assistant secretaries.

By the end of the Reagan administration's first year, the period of this
study, most of the conflicts I witnessed were between political appointees,
usually within an agency. I cannot recall, for example, hearing the White
House mentioned when I was in the FDA press office or the FDA mentioned
when I was in the White House press office. They were simply too far outside
each other's field of vision. There were titanic struggles between the secretary
of state and the national security adviser, of course, but this level of combat

involved very few government workers. Most fights turn out to be not us against them but us against us, including some internecine quarrels among career personnel.[9]

Of the patterns of loyalty I observed, political appointees could be most loyal to career officers or career officers could be most loyal to political appointees; people tended to be most loyal to those who were their immediate supervisors. Therefore, it would be a mistake to determine the organizational location of press offices on the basis of whether employees are career personnel. Rather, organizers must weigh the gain that might come from consolidating all press operations of the subunits at the top or agency level— "speaking with one voice"—against the loss in knowledgeability and currency that would come from increasing the distance between press officers and the sources in the bureaucracy of the information that they are expected to be able to explain to the news media. In large agencies the decision is usually (and correctly I think) made to decentralize, to maintain press operations in all of the important subunits.[10]

Given the common situation in which subunit press officers are often more loyal to their administrators than to their department's public affairs director, however, problems of control caused by decentralizing press operations are real and can be serious for those at the top. Whatever power the department press office has over the news generated in the subunits comes from its oversight of routine responsibilities—approving press releases and clearing speeches—and from favors, persuasion, and, most important, the backing of the cabinet officer, as in the following examples from the Department of Transportation:

—A subunit administrator wants to put out a press release praising a nongovernmental report favorable to his unit. He argues that the publicity would be good for the morale of his employees. The department press chief argues that it is a puff piece and that issuing it would mean a loss of credibility with reporters. The department head decides in favor of the press chief, and the draft release is not issued.

—Another subunit administrator wants to do a television interview on the use of human cadavers in research. The department press chief thinks it is in poor taste. The department head again decides in favor of his press chief, and the interview is canceled.

Generally, the press operations strategy of the subunits is to stay out of their department's sight as much as possible. There are times, of course, when they solicit help—when a story needs a cabinet official as the drawing card, for example—but usually they see themselves as responding to the demands that departments' secretaries make upon them, and these can differ dramatically. At the FDA, for example, press office veterans recall Joseph Califano (1977–79) as being more involved in their activities than any other HEW (HHS) chief, David Mathews (1975–77) as having little interest in press relations, and Patricia Harris (1979–81) as being in-between, meaning, they say, that their activities were approved as long as there were no surprises.

Occasionally a subunit chooses to be insubordinate. If higher powers notice and object, it may apologize, but more often the subunit simply denies the insubordination. It looked as if the Coast Guard press office were being insubordinate when Transportation Secretary Drew Lewis tried to cut the Coast Guard budget in January 1982. Newspaper headlines proclaimed, SEA SERVICES IMPERILED (Baltimore *Sun*) and POSSIBLE COAST GUARD MERGER BRINGS WAVE OF PROTESTS (*Journal of Commerce*). Yet reporters assure me that the Coast Guard's feeble press operation would not have been capable of waging this campaign. Instead, with considerable skill the Coast Guard commandant had executed the so-called Washington Monument Game, proposing to cut the most popular programs. Headlines then correctly reflected howls from members of Congress.[11]

DURING CRISES, which are the subject of another chapter, conditions are often so unpredictable and chaotic that a press office's response may seem to reflect a thorough absence of organization. But somewhere on the scale between crises and routine activities are events that might be called routine crises—a revolution, for instance, that might affect international alignments of power or the safety of American nationals. These events recur regularly enough that they can be and are planned for. Such situations most often confront the Defense Department and the State Department, which have adopted markedly different organizational methods for their press offices to respond to them, procedures that tend to have contrasting effects on press coverage and press relations.

On August 19, 1981, at 7:45 a.m., Defense Secretary Weinberger told a hastily convened press conference, "Two United States Navy F-14 aircraft, involved in a previously announced routine exercise in international airspace over international waters in the south central Mediterranean, were attacked early this morning by two Libyan SU-22 fighter aircraft. After being fired upon, the F-14s, based on the U.S. aircraft carrier *Nimitz*, took action in response and shot down both Libyan aircraft at 1:20 a.m." In the six-and-a-half hours between the shootout and the announcement, the Pentagon prepared a fact sheet for internal use consisting of twenty-three questions that reporters were likely to ask and an approved answer for each, among them:

Q. History of activities in Gulf of Sidra?
A. There have been eight routine naval exercises conducted in this area since July 1977 without incident, the last in September of 1980.
Q. Description of exercise?
A. The exercise was a two-day scheduled missile readiness exercise involving ships and aircraft of the Sixth Fleet, firing surface-to-air missiles and air-to-air missiles at target drones.
Q. How many times were interceptions made before this action?
A. During the first day of the exercise, there were thirty-six interceptions of unidentified aircraft.
Q. What weapons did the Libyan aircraft fire at the U.S. aircraft?
A. The Libyans fired one missile at the U.S. [F-14]. The other Libyan aircraft was maneuvering for a firing position.
Q. What weapons did the U.S. aircraft fire?
A. The U.S. aircraft fired the Sidewinder missile.

The Pentagon was organized for the wholesale dissemination of information. There could be as many press officers as there were telephones. All reporters calling in were guaranteed fast service, the same basic information, and no more.

The State Department, on the other hand, chooses a retail organizational strategy when confronted with a routine crisis. Whether it is the Polish government declaring martial law or a war between Britain and Argentina over the Falkland Islands, the crisis gets reassigned from the bureau of the region in which the event has taken place to a specially constructed task force. The Pentagon's wholesale strategy adds press officers; the State Department's retail strategy subtracts them: there are more press officers in the Bureau of Inter-American Affairs (Argentina) and the Bureau of European Affairs (Great Britain) than there were in the Falklands Working Group.

The quality of the press officer is almost irrelevant in the wholesale strategy because there can be no deviation from the written responses. In the retail strategy, the quality of the press officer is more important. But regardless of that quality, bottlenecks must develop as more and more reporters seek information. Ultimately, then, the State Department's format disseminates less information, which, of course, may be the reason the department chooses this design. The resulting constriction of access, however, forces reporters to go elsewhere for answers—usually to congressional committees, foreign embassies, or other reporters—and the information that gets broadcast or published is, from the State Department's vantage point, less reliable.

ORGANIZATION for the routine crisis is a special case, of course. For routine daily operations most government press offices arrange their work load in much the same manner as a newspaper's Washington bureau of comparable size. If the bureau is very small, the division of labor tends to be highly informal and the worker is apt to be a generalist. As the operation grows, it acquires structure. Each press officer gets a beat (called an "account" at the Pentagon). At the FDA, for example, press officers' assignments include food, cosmetics, drugs, biologics, veterinary medicine, medical devices, and radiation. Drugs and food are the premier beats; entering press officers are more likely to be given veterinary medicine or medical devices.

Just as in a newsroom, the pecking order of beats within a government agency depends on a subject's visibility and potential for excitement. Reporters and press officers both want to avoid the dull and boring assignments. However, a young Pentagon reporter who offers the opinion that the work of a government press officer is boring does not seem to notice the irony that most of his workday is spent waiting for government officials to see him or answer his calls. Fortunately for purposes of organizational maintenance, not every press officer or reporter gets excited by the same stimuli. An FDA press officer who compiles *Enforcement Report*, a weekly listing of prosecutions, seizures, recalls, and injunctions, finds it "pretty interesting. This week we will have a recall of crab meat."

The system of covering beats reaches the proportions of three-dimensional chess at the Pentagon's Armed Forces News branch, where army, navy, and air force press officers each have three accounts: their military branch, a geographic area, and a substantive assignment. A lieutenant colonel, for instance, may be responsible for the army, North Africa and the Middle East, and atomic energy, space operations, and security assistance. If a member of the U.S. army is shot by a Korean in Korea, answering reporters' questions will be the responsibility of the press officer with the Korea account (a navy lientenant commander), but if the soldier is shot by another U.S. soldier, questions go to the army desk. A question on Bright Star, a military exercise in the Middle East, was given to the press officer who handled rapid deployment forces, even though his geographic account was the Caribbean. The rule of thumb seems to be that substance outranks geography, which outranks service branch. "The action precedence," says news chief James Freeman, "becomes instinctive." Moreover, since military people have a firm understanding of hierarchy, few jurisdictional disputes erupt, and there is always someone of a higher rank to straighten them out.

HOW MUCH does one press operation resemble another? This was the question I asked myself as I left the FDA, the smallest press office I examined and the first stop on my five-agency tour, and crossed the Potomac to the Pentagon. After all, the Defense Department produces nearly twelve times as many news releases a year as the FDA. I expected to find that scale was going to be a determinant in my assessment.

Not necessarily so, I discovered. Neither quality nor responsiveness seemed to me to be directly related to size. I found differences in personnel, but again the distinctions were not based on whether an agency was large or small. There were also some differences in techniques among the agencies—in the way briefings were conducted, for example (briefings are discussed in a separate chapter). And the location of an agency seemed to have an effect on the nature of its operation. The FDA is in Rockville, Maryland; marginal reporters do not drop by as they often do at the State Department in downtown Washington. One reporter, who is known for asking odd questions, told me that he always goes to the State Department when he is having a slow day. In this regard, noted an FDA press officer, "Geography serves us well." As for reorganizations of press offices, sometimes I saw them as ways to get rid of employees who perform poorly or who cause trouble, but this management trick is not unique to press operations.

Given that all press offices share the generic characteristics of servicing the news media, perhaps I should not have been surprised to find that regardless of how they were organized or how different their sizes, each performed the same duties in a similar manner. Indeed, it becomes possible to generalize in this study exactly because the Pentagon's press operation appears much like the FDA's writ large.

CHAPTER 3

Press Secretaries
and Career Press Officers

WHAT MAKES the most difference in the proper functioning of press offices, reporters rightly note, is the quality of the people who work in them, their ability, interest, and dedication. But personal ability is not the only criterion. Success or failure of a press operation also depends on relationships between types of personnel, between the press secretaries or spokesmen who come to government with a new president and the career press officers whose service spans presidential administrations. Other important relationships, and often more subtle ones, are those between press secretaries and the political echelons of their agencies and between career press officers and the permanent bureaucracies of the same agencies.

Reporters believe that what makes a good press secretary is access, the perceived closeness to the head of the agency. They will tolerate most faults, even arrogance, if they think the spokesman has access. And although they appreciate such virtues as kindness in a press secretary, that appreciation will not change their assessment of his usefulness if they do not think he has access. That he has good access is the highest compliment a reporter can pay a press secretary. As the AP's Fred Hoffman said of Defense Department spokesman Thomas Ross, "he would pick up the phone and call [Defense Secretary] Brown at any time." The position of press secretary exists largely because reporters cannot speak to policymakers whenever they feel the need.[1]

There is no litmus test that can determine whether an official and the person hired to speak for him will form a close relationship. It should be assumed that the boss will have a boss-sized ego and that the spokesman chosen to represent him should be prepared to stay as faceless as possible. One careful observer of Jimmy Carter's White House said that both National Security Adviser Zbigniew Brzezinski and his first press aide, Jerrold Schechter, "wanted their pictures taken at the best parties." Such competition for

18

the limelight is no formula for a lasting friendship, and that did not remain one.[2] As a rule of thumb, employer and employee should not be prominently before the press at the same time; the subordinate can be prominent only if the principal declines the honor, as did Cyrus Vance when he allowed and possibly even encouraged Hodding Carter to assume an unusually conspicuous public persona. The same rule of thumb was echoed by Wayne Pines, the FDA press chief, when he told me that his boss, the FDA commissioner, should not get more publicity than the Health and Human Services secretary under whom he serves. Obviously a president will never be upstaged by his press secretary in quantity of attention given him, but that is not necessarily true of others in an administration. If a press secretary is getting better publicity than his employer, the employer has a right to wonder whether his subordinate has gone into business for himself.

Given the importance of this relationship, it might be assumed that the head of an agency would personally pick his spokesman. Yet below the presidential level this happens less often than expected. Every White House personnel office likes to impose press chiefs on the agencies. A president-elect may owe few campaign debts to nuclear physicists or Russian-speaking would-be diplomats, but he will have no shortage of people with press and public relations backgrounds to whom he is grateful and who now wish to join his government. In theory, imposing press chiefs on agencies is a bad system because it demands instant rapport between total strangers. In practice it works about as well as if the head of the agency picks the spokesman. Some of the best press secretaries were previously unknown to their superior officials; other officials picked their own spokesmen and were not as fortunate. This situation may reflect the reality that many new agency heads come to Washington having limited acquaintance with people who would be good press secretaries and little appreciation of what a good one should be doing for them.

No special set of personality traits is considered mandatory in a press secretary. It usually helps to have a sense of humor, although a ready wit is not always a blessing. One reporter said he admired the way Henry Catto at the Pentagon could deflect a question with a joke, while another said he resented it, implying that national defense was a subject too serious for joking. In recent years there have been a large number of press secretaries who seem to have profited from appearing to be relaxed, low key, and easy going. Often they are from the South and work hard at maintaining the image of a good old boy. Admonishing reporters about their treatment of a fellow Mississippian, Larry Speakes said, "don't you be on to him. He's a nice fella. Talks funny, but he's nice." Yet the presidential press secretary considered the best ever, Eisenhower's James Hagerty, was a New Yorker with none of these personal qualities. (Besides having access, Hagerty was the first White House press secretary noted for attention to logistical detail, the minute-by-minute planning of events, which is now taken for granted.)

Techniques and other aspects of the job can be learned and honed through practice. "You should have seen him six months ago" was a comment I heard from reporters wherever there was a relatively new spokesman. In time the spokesman learns a great deal about the reporters. A former State Department briefer soon realized that a particular reporter was more apt to make a speech than ask a question and learned to call on him only after all the other reporters had had a turn. There are also lessons to be learned about an agency's personnel. A press officer at the FDA commented, "after two years here I know who I can put on TV and who I can't. It's scary to be on TV if you're not trained to do it. Channel 2 in New York called yesterday for an interview on caffeine. I knew not to ask the scientists. So I got Sandy Miller [director of the FDA's Bureau of Foods], who is good at this sort of thing." Then too, reporters grow accustomed to press secretaries. They learn from daily exposure that certain phrases and mannerisms are expected to have certain meanings. Perhaps the spokesman has not improved on some objective scale, but misunderstandings become less likely. This suggests that agencies would be wise not to change press secretaries more often than is absolutely necessary.

But most reporters who comment on a press secretary's improvement on the job simply mean that he has become more familiar with the agency's business. The new spokesman usually knows less about the subject and operation of an agency than many of the reporters he is expected to inform. This point is illustrated in columnist Philip Geyelin's interview with Hodding Carter after he had left government:[3]

> Geyelin: When you came to the State Department, how much exposure had you had to the sort of things you were going to be dealing with?
> Carter: Essentially not very much. I'd been to the Soviet Union a couple of times and South Africa several times, and Europe a number of times. I'd gone to the Woodrow Wilson School [at Princeton] with the idea of going into the Foreign Service, but I wound up back in Greenville [Mississippi] running the family newspaper instead. Things that sort of semiqualified me were being a member of the Atlantic Association of Young Political Leaders and the American Council of Young Political Leaders.

The press secretary does not have to be a substantive expert; he rarely is, and it is not expected of him. But he had best be a quick study.

When a large part of the press secretary's job is to conduct briefings—twice a day at the White House, once a day at the State Department, twice a week at Defense in peacetime—reporters expect him to be articulate. But after having observed at least a hundred briefings during the year, I concluded that it is not exactly verbal skill that they are looking for. David Gergen, surely one of the most verbally precise people to serve as a White House spokesman, was not a popular briefer; reporters found him too professorial. He was replaced on a regular basis by Larry Speakes, who came close to conducting briefings in mime—shrugging, gesturing with his hands, raising eyebrows, lowering eyes. His sentences did not always parse, but reporters judged him an acceptable performer. In general, by the way, body language has become an important part of the ritual. A reporter turned to me after a briefing by State Department spokesman Dean Fischer and, referring triumphantly to a question he had asked, said, "Did you notice his vacant stare, as if he didn't understand? *He understood.*" To have thought that Fischer simply had not understood would have ruined the reporter's fun. What reporters appreciate in a briefer and what they seem subconsciously to look for is that he share their love of the game.

Reporters also say that they want a spokesman to be evenhanded. This does not mean that they expect to be treated alike. They understand the distinctions among news organizations and types of media, that reporters have varying deadlines and need different kinds of information. They accept the reality that there will be exclusives, times when a competitor is given a break on a story. Rather, what they mean is that among reporters representing comparable and competing organizations or reporters covering news at the same levels of sophistication, a good press secretary will, in the words of the *Boston Globe*'s William Beecher, "conduct himself in a manner that leaves each reporter with a sense that his turn will come." When Alexander Haig gave an exclusive interview to reporters from the *New York Times*, the *Washington Post*, *Time*, and *Newsweek*, other print reporters in the State Department pressroom grumbled for days, even though Haig had not revealed anything that they considered interesting; on the other hand, the television network reporters did not complain, possibly because they had all been excluded.

In choosing government press secretaries, officials and personnel offices automatically gravitate toward journalists. After all, who knows more about deadlines and the logistical needs of the news media, about the elements of a good story and the personalities of those in the press corps? In practice, however, some good journalists have become weak press secretaries. Part of the reason may be that journalists think journalism is a higher calling. If so, they may enter government service with a sense that they are selling out or demeaning themselves, what a Pentagon reporter calls "the nun going over the wall" and a State Department reporter calls "joining the enemy." Reporters will make a moral exception for colleagues who join government at a high enough level, especially if they plan to return to journalism. Commenting on Eileen Shanahan, who left the *New York Times* to become assistant secretary for public affairs in the Department of Health, Education, and Welfare during the Carter administration, another *Times* reporter said, "I think I reflect the newsroom in saying that we felt she was moving into a really responsible position." But while reporters think there is a special cachet to diplomatic service, even in the form of a modest ambassadorship, only a top appointment in a very large agency on the domestic side of government, as in Shanahan's case, would be thought respectable enough for a *Times* person by members of the *Times* Washington bureau.[4]

Press secretaries who had been reporters were the ones most likely to tell me that reporters ask shallow questions or do not do their homework. "I'm surprised at how little the press corps demand sometimes; my estimation of them has gone down," said a former reporter after two years in government. Such criticisms might be explained in psychological terms or as based on a new understanding of the complexities inside government. Some reporters-turned-spokesmen also justify themselves to themselves on the grounds that their new work is not so very different. They pass along most information with no spin on it; like the reporters they were, their objective is still to send forth accurate and useful information, the bulk of which—a contract awarded, a commission established, an official appointed—is basic and uncontroversial. But beyond the bare bones of fact—at the point where a good reporter asks "why?"—the interests of reporter and press secretary begin to diverge, and the press secretary must weigh the ramifications for his employer. A press secretary is not simply a misplaced reporter who happens to have wandered over to the other side of the podium.

Probably the spokesmen who experience the fewest conflicts over loyalties are those who have made press relations their business. A number of presidential press secretaries—James Hagerty, George Christian, Jody Powell—had been press secretaries to governors.[5] There is also an occasional internal promotion. The four key spokesmen at the Reagan White House in 1982—David Gergen, Larry Speakes, Peter Roussel, and Lyndon (Mort) Allin—had served on the Nixon or Ford White House staffs, suggesting perhaps that there is a growing cadre of professional political spokesmen, one by-product of the chain of brief presidencies.

Is any background a predictor of success or failure as a government press chief? A career press officer, mulling over the many bosses he had worked for, finally concluded that he could not answer my question. He had seen them come from journalism, business, and politics; they had been good and not very good, in no pattern that related to previous occupation. Perhaps no other work was exactly comparable. Someone from corporate public relations might be uneasy with the degree of openness that is expected in government press relations; someone from journalism might be uneasy with the amount of government activity that legitimately should be closed to the press. Someone coming from a political campaign might find that the responsibility of speaking for those who are accountable for governing imposes unnatural restraints; someone coming from the government career service might be less of an advocate than a political executive has the right to expect.[6]

PRESS SECRETARIES, even when they are career press officers, as occasionally happens, must act as surrogates for a president or one of his appointees and therefore perform an essentially political function. They are hired to present their employer—the person and the agency—in as favorable a light as possible. "Inevitably you serve as an advocate," says Eileen Shanahan. "It is a question of honest advocacy."[7]

There are certain rules of honest advocacy, although there are still disputes over what constitutes ethical conduct, in part because government public relations is a relatively new business. When conventions of attribution are not precisely defined and widely accepted, for example, there are misunderstandings and charges of bad faith. As an internal memorandum* from its press office that circulated throughout the State Department in 1982 reported, "considerable confusion exists regarding the ground rules for conversations with reporters. . . . What exactly does 'background' mean? What is 'deep background'? When can one be quoted and when should one's remarks be attributed to 'an Administration official'?"[8]

Reporters often fall back on game-playing analogies when discussing these interactions; the analogous sports are of the controlled-combat variety, such as football. While there is a growing body of rules to be obeyed, players occasionally choose to break a rule if they feel that there is little risk of getting caught or if they estimate that the rewards outweigh the cost in penalties. For example, if a White House pool reporter breaks the rule that he must never file a story for his own use before sharing it with colleagues, his penalty is to be singled out in conversation as the reporter who broke the

*See "Documents," p. 118.

rule. But there is no appointed referee or umpire nor is there likely to be, partly for constitutional reasons, partly because players on both sides think they gain an advantage by unsupervised play.

For all press secretaries the crux of ethical conduct is lying. Spokesmen are expected to tell the truth—it is U.S. government policy. They also prefer to tell the truth; to lie is to fail to play fair with reporters and the public, to diminish their self-esteem, and to complicate their work. But spokesmen are also expected to support the administration, which in turn is expected to act in the best interests of the American people, and that may sometimes require withholding full information. Reporters understand these conditions, and the conventions of the government/press connection permit less than full candor. Acceptability, however, depends on the kind of lie and its extent. On a scale of decreasing acceptability to reporters, the types would be the honest lie, the inadvertent lie, the half-truth, and the lie.

When a group of former presidential press secretaries appearing before reporters in the White House briefing room on April 23, 1982, were asked if they had ever lied to the press, two admitted they had. Ron Nessen confessed that he had once said President Ford was going to Florida to "inspect a weather plane" when his trip was "primarily to play in a golf tournament." President Carter's spokesman, Jody Powell, said he lied "to protect the Iranian rescue mission."[9] Powell's honest lie would be considered justifiable by most Washington reporters. A year-and-a-half later *Washington Post* reporter Lois Romano asked former presidential press secretaries what they might have said or not said to reporters in order to protect the secrecy of the U.S. invasion of Grenada in October 1983, another instance that could have called for an honest lie. Among their suggestions:

> *Ron Nessen:* "I don't have anything to give you on that."
> *Bill Moyers:* "Now if you were me, would you feel comfortable telling you?"
> *Jody Powell:* "Just blabber on and on with things like 'I don't know, the men haven't confided in me.'"
> *Pierre Salinger,* recalling a similar experience: "I just disappeared for the evening."[10]

To date, cases in which press secretaries offered honest lies have involved national security considerations, but it is conceivable that officials in the future will find other types of actions—impending devaluation of the currency, for instance, or monetary decisions that could lead to hoarding—that would require deception on the part of their spokesmen for "the public good."[11]

Somewhere between the acceptable lie and the half-truth is the inadvertent lie. "At times circumstances make a liar out of you," recalls Bill Moyers;

and looking back on some past crises, a Pentagon press officer commented, "these are the days that the phones are jumping off the hook. At the end of the day you have a good feeling that you've helped to explain the story and a prayer that you're telling the truth." Good reporters sympathize with this; they too have the same feeling. Truthfulness in the government/press connection is limited by the possible and the present. The tacit understanding is that information given today could turn out to be wrong tomorrow. But inadvertent lies may provide more frustrations than other types because they are more common. According to William Beecher, who served under Defense Secretary James Schlesinger, "half of the initial internal reporting within government in a crisis is wrong."

At the April 23, 1982, session with reporters, Jody Powell noted, "I was pretty good at treading that line between intentionally misleading and lying." Or as a British Foreign Office spokesman remarked to a reporter: "You think we lie to you. But we don't lie, really we don't. However, when you discover that, you make an even greater error. You think we tell you the truth."[12] On our scale, these are the half-truths. In my year of wanderig between officials and reporters, I watched the phenomenon many times. Sometimes I thought I saw the line crossed, although the incidents all involved small matters. The press secretary's technique is almost always to define the question as narrowly as possible, as in these semihypothetical examples:

Q. Has the assistant secretary of state been invited to China?
A. No. (Meaning: *He will go to China as an adviser to the vice president. It is the vice president who will be invited. Therefore, I am not lying.* Rationale: *I have to say this because protocol requires that the Chinese must first publicly extend the invitation.*)

Q. Will the ambassador-at-large go to Egypt?
A. No decision has been made. (Meaning: *A "decision" is made when the secretary of state signs the cable. The cable will be signed tomorrow. Therefore, I am not lying.* Rationale: *I do not have the authority to give a premature confirmation.*)

It is by unraveling the half-truths that reporters display their professional skill; consequently, they too have a vested interest in maintaining this system despite whatever personal beliefs they have about government's obligation to tell the truth.

It is only the Big Lie, the deliberate and consistent pattern of misstatement on a matter of importance, that turns Washington reporters into inflamed civil libertarians. Some journalists feel that this pattern was characteristic of the government during the Vietnam years: a distinguished reporter, now retired, recalls, "I was lied to every goddam day." But this harsh assessment may fail to give proper weighting to the confusion of wartime, expecially in communications between headquarters and the field. Jerry W. Friedheim, an assistant secretary of defense for public affairs during the period, comments that reporters' recollections "are mostly war stories. . . . It was hotter in Saigon for military briefers who could not answer policy questions than it was for me at the Pentagon. . . . I briefed every day for six years and didn't lie. . . . And someplace in accounts of Vietnam it needs to be mentioned always that there was no censorship."[13]

To SERVE effectively as an honest advocate for a political executive and his policies, a press secretary must be "in the loop," Washington parlance for being included in the inner circle where alternative actions are debated, decisions concluded, and plans formulated. When a press secretary's statements turn out to be untrue or misleading, what appears at best to be a calculated half-truth may actually be a kind of inadvertent lie because the secretary had been kept in the dark by a superior. The conduct of Ron Ziegler is instructive: during the Watergate period he did not lie to the press; he simply did not know the facts. (This case is extreme in that to have known the facts could have been an indictable offense.) It is common practice in government—or at least a common excuse—for bosses not to keep their press spokesmen informed so as to protect them from having to lie. When I saw this happen in the Reagan administration, it was not because higher-ups expected spokesmen to lie, but rather that they suspected them as the sources of leaks. When reporters were called back to the White House on the afternoon of June 25, 1982, the press officers doing the phoning did not know the briefing would announce that Alexander Haig was to be replaced as secretary of state by George Shultz.

Since press secretaries know that it is the sine qua non of spokesmanship to be in the loop, they sometimes exaggerate the degree of their involvement in top-level decisions. But there are certain unmistakable clues that indicate a spokesman's standing:

—an office close by the boss's,

—being constantly in the boss's presence (especially when riding in a car, since there are fewer seats than in a plane),

—being invited to meetings that are beyond a spokesman's job description, such as hiring and firing persons other than press officers,

—having people of higher rank in the agency come to the spokesman's office.

A press officer at the FDA bemoans "the symbolism that we're not on the same floor as the executive offices." However, Morton Lebow, a former public affairs director of the Public Health Service, which fits above the FDA on the HHS organizational chart, questions whether office location has any effect at the FDA. His attitude is most likely the result of working for an agency that receives relatively little sustained attention from the mass media. For example, when Herbert Kaufman studied the activities of the heads of such government units as the Customs Service, the Forest Service, and the Internal Revenue Service, he found that they were "likely to have only a few media contacts a month. Consequently . . . this was not [among] their most demanding duties. They never took it lightly, but it was not a principal consumer of their time."[14]

The rule of propinquity also breaks down in agencies that have a pressroom. Where reporters remain on the premises, two government axioms are in conflict: one that the press secretary should be near the reporters, the other that the reporters should be removed from the immediate vicinity of the principal officials. The latter takes precedence, thus pushing the spokesman away from his boss. The State Department attempts to solve the dilemma of appearance by giving the press secretary the use of two offices, one on the second floor with the press and one on the sixth floor with the other assistant secretaries or the seventh floor when the spokesman is not an assistant secretary.

A typical configuration by function of those in the loop, in roughly the order of endearment to the boss, could be friend, secretary, lawyer, administrator, press secretary. Often a person assumes more than one role, thereby freeing a seat in what may become a game of musical chairs. When the music stops, the press secretary's seat is usually the first to be yanked, probably because as troubles mount, his ability and even his loyalty are most easily called into question. George Reedy, one of Lyndon Johnson's press secretaries, commented that "no president can find it within his ego to concede that he failed in any degree with the public. It is far more satisfying to blame his failures on the press."[15] Reedy could have added, "and the press secretary."

Having the spokesman in the loop does not ensure wise or popular policy, of course. President Johnson created a war cabinet that met on Tuesdays to review Vietnam developments. Besides the president, its six regular members were the secretaries of state and defense, the NSC adviser, the CIA director, the chairman of the Joint Chiefs of Staff, and the White House press secretary (first Bill Moyers, then George Christian).[16] And in Jimmy Carter's administration, voted out of office, press secretary Jody Powell was rated one of the two most influential members of the White House staff.[17] Moreover, the term *news management* was invented in 1955 when James Hagerty was press secretary and was an intimate of the president.[18]

Only one of the five spokesmen I followed would I judge to have been in the loop; other interviews suggest that one in five would be a reasonable reflection of the entire executive branch. "More often than not," says David H. Brown, a veteran press officer, "we are after-the-fact implementers [rather] than predecision inputers." Perhaps one reason I witnessed so little successful government manipulation of the news media in 1981–82 was because skilled press officers were usually far removed from the inner ring. Consequently the attempts to manipulate the press—mostly through leaks—were made by political officials, often with simplistic and misguided notions of the news media.

The paradox, then, of the spokesman's ultimate role as counselor, advising executives on what is likely to be the perception of what they are planning to do as refracted through the media, is that it could increase the possibilities of controlling the news.

THE PRESS SECRETARY of a new president moves into the White House with a staff of eager young loyalists who have been campaign assistants, while at the departments and agencies the new press secretaries arrive alone and are greeted by career personnel who, assuming continued correct conduct as defined by civil service regulations, are the government's present and future press officers.

Most spokesmen bridle at this inheritance. They feel hemmed in by their inability to hire and fire. They repeat bad luck stories—"I have a press officer who sits in his office all day serving imaginary tennis balls." Political appointees also suspect the loyalty of these permanent employees, especially if the outgoing administration has been of the other party. Nor is the suspicion always paranoid. Some career personnel do have an ideology that may peep out from under the veneer of professionalism.[19] As one military press officer said about working for a dovish administration, "We were laggards, not disloyal."

Career personnel, on the other hand, worry that the new people are going to politicize information. Early in the Kennedy administration, for example, the special assistant to the secretary of commerce circulated a memorandum telling the department's bureaus that "in making announcements of local projects, the President should be given a credit line in the lead paragraph."[20]

Politicizing information has nothing to do, however, with stories of high political content or other stories that have the potential to cause trouble for an administration because of the controversial nature of the subject. It is expected that these stories will routinely be bucked from the career officers to their politically appointed superiors. When a young FDA press officer was called by an Associated Press reporter after Dr. Denton Cooley had performed an artificial heart transplant in July 1981, he offered the opinion that "the surgeon should have submitted an application [to the FDA] for permission to use the device." Cooley responded that he had no time to bother with red tape when a patient was dying.[21] Ultimately the FDA reviewed the case and decided that its press officer's reaction had been correct, but the agency's press chief, convening his staff, told them that in such situations the correct response to a reporter should have been "I'll get back to you"—after checking with higher authorities. The experienced career officer learns to sense when the routine has the potential to turn controversial or political and, rightly, tosses it to the press secretary as if it were a ticking time bomb.

Eventually press secretaries sort out the talents of the career personnel, learn which ones to rely on, and often discover abilities that they had not originally imagined. They learn when personnel regulations can be bent to their advantage (usually in hiring) and when it is not worth the effort (usually in firing). The caution of the bureaucracy, which they first view as pusillanimity, begins to look like a sensible device for keeping the agency out of trouble. In internal debates over whether to respond to a bothersome story, for example, the vote for letting it pass usually comes from the press officer, who, if overruled, often turns out to be right. As one spokesman noted, "I had a low estimation of the press officers when I got here. I now think they've handled some matters skillfully, and, most important, they haven't caused any flaps."

And as for the fear that press officers will be disloyal? At one agency I saw a career officer writing political speeches for a Republican official; in the previous administration he had written political speeches for a Democratic official. "I think I should do whatever I can to make [the official's] life easier. Also I enjoy it and it helps me survive." Bureaucrats have the most to gain by providing satisfactory service.

Who are these press officers, these public affairs bureaucrats, the people syndicated columnist Marianne Means contended would never be missed? There is a notion—widely believed among journalists—that, in the words of one reporter, press officers "are tired burnt-out newsmen who flunked on this side of the street." But fewer than half the press officers I met had worked for news organizations long enough to be thought of as ex-journalists: four of nine at the FDA, for example. Nevertheless, many public information officers stressed their journalism experience when I interviewed them, perhaps a reflection of the prestige accorded reporters; one with extensive training in public administration talked instead about his days on the campus radio station. Their resumes made clear, however, that many had merely dabbled at journalism while in college, or for a short time after college, or part time—hardly long enough to burn out.

I did meet some former reporters and editors who had worked for fifteen years or more at news organizations, sometimes jumping from job to job, and who now seemed embarrassed to have been discovered in the employ of government, or at least talked about having joined government as if it had been an accident—*My paper folded . . . My wife had another child . . . My managing editor was an S.O.B.* Several struck me as very good press officers, among the best I observed. They also carried with them into government service a trait I had often seen when studying veteran newsmen—habitual complaining—which in either occupation rarely interfered with job performance. Only one of the former reporters I watched could qualify as a burnt-out case, although he probably had never been on fire.

By the time I met them, many former reporters had spent more years as press officers than as journalists. Increasingly they had come to consider government information work as a career, not simply something to do between other jobs. They called themselves communicators, and like those in other occupations reaching out to bolster status, they paid dues to professional-sounding societies, held seminars, wrote codes of conduct, gave themselves awards for distinguished service, and stressed educational credentials.

The number of advanced degrees among Pentagon press officers was particularly impressive. An Army major had a Ph.D. in education; a lieutenant colonel was working on a Ph.D. in Byzantine history; a colonel was getting his second M.A. This, of course, tends to be a characteristic of the armed services rather than just of press offices. Since there must be an oversupply of military manpower in peacetime, educational training becomes one way of absorbing the time of standby personnel. But even at the FDA, where the press officers had paid for their own schooling, there were three M.A.s (in journalism, public administration, and biology) on the nine-person staff.

In terms of educational background, Washington reporters seemed to get their undergraduate degrees from more elite institutions than did career press officers; I found reporters, but no career press officers, who had attended Ivy League schools.[22] The reporters were also more likely to have completed graduate studies before beginning a full-time career and were more likely to have terminal degrees, most often in law, although this was a very small percentage in both groups.[23] Press officers were more apt to do their graduate work at night or on government time at universities in the Washington area, and were much more likely to have pursued a vocational course of study. Fewer than half the reporters with advanced degrees had earned them in journalism. The irony of the career officers' accent on communication skills was that those I talked with did not think that what they had studied had measurably improved their job performance.[24] What improved, they were quick to admit, were their chances for advancement in grade. "The more boxes you have checked the better. They don't ask you what you've learned."

My impression is that press officers put in more than the normal number of hours for government workers of comparable rank. In part this is because press operations maintain a duty-officer system. Someone is available at all times, including evenings and weekends, with the frequency of the assignment depending on the number of people on the roster. After a "relatively quiet night" a Pentagon duty officer said he had had eight calls from reporters, the last one coming shortly before midnight (the biggest story was about the forced retirement of Admiral Rickover). "It's busier on the weekends when less experienced reporters are on and they need to ask more questions." A weekend duty officer at the State Department said she had received fifty calls and had answered most queries with "no comment." "Reporters must have known that this would be the case. I suspect that they were calling so that they could tell their editors, if asked, that they had called." Some extra hours are the result of crises, but more often press officers work overtime because they service a very demanding and sometimes arrogant clientele. Reporters call in from different time zones. "They're so inconsiderate," said the State Department duty officer, who had been awakened on a Friday night by queries from an out-of-town reporter about a story that was several weeks old. A press pass seems to turn some people into bullies; they act toward underlings in a manner that they would not dare act toward high-ranking officials. This, at least, is the way the government/press connection sometimes looks to the person behind the desk.[25] One press officer at the White House thinks that, even more than civility, what he needs in order to do his job well is "to like reporters."

Press offices also maintain a system of staggered shifts. In addition to trying to stretch the business day as much as possible, they need to have the news stories that have appeared since 5:00 p.m. the previous day in a digested, summarized, or otherwise processed form by the time the rest of the government workers arrive in the morning. Some press officers are at their desks before 7:00 a.m. and others are there after 7:00 p.m. These odd hours, like those associated with police work, the entertainment industry, and journalism, may add to the press officers' sense of apartness. Those government workers who do not maintain a nine-to-five schedule, I suspect, are less likely to see themselves as bureaucrats. Their work, however, does not involve much travel. Although the permanent people in the State Department press office, for example, may go to New York City for an occasional session of the UN General Assembly, they never get the exotic trips that are assigned to upwardly mobile reporters.

Press officers seem to enjoy their relatively nonbureaucratic hours and duties, in part because their jobs often require them to step outside the normal channels of their organizations. They have much more contact with officials in the highest strata of government than do other civil servants of the same grade. A naval lieutenant commander described his role as press officer during one crisis: "I was talking with the chairman of the Joint Chiefs of Staff," he said excitedly. "Now that's a short chain of command!" They also enjoy occasional moments of public recognition. "By turning the dial I heard myself simultaneously on three stations." "Sometimes you make a statement and an hour later you see it on the wires." These comments by different career officers were delivered with obvious pleasure. "When I played baseball as a kid, I always wanted to play first base. That's where whatever action there is passes by. It's the same with press relations."

The occasional prestige, however, does not translate into higher status. In places where government personnel systems have an elite, press officers are not thought of as being in it by those who are in it. In the words of a report on the comparable distinction made in the British government, press officers are "equal and below."[26] At the Pentagon, for instance, all colonels may be equal, but the colonel who is a press officer is rarely a product of West Point or Annapolis, never one of what a veteran reporter called "the water walkers." Many of those I met had become career personnel after serving in the armed forces reserves or even the National Guard.[27] At the FDA, a scientific establishment, most of the press officers commented ruefully on their lack of scientific training. A Foreign Service officer in the State Department's press office noted that the assignment was not useful to her career, although she found it interesting. The director of public affairs at the Agency for International Development, Kate Semerad, said she had difficulties trying to recruit Foreign Service people for her office because they see public affairs as "a diversion (perhaps a permanent one) from their career goal."[28] Some Foreign Service officers in the State Department hinted to me of a subtle distinction in status between themselves and those in the U.S.

Information Agency who serve as the public affairs officers in our embassies; USIA officers deny this with more vigor than would be necessary if there were no differences.[29]

All reporters also feel superior to all career press officers.[30] Otherwise why is it that some reporters who fall from grace become press officers but no career press officers rise from the ashes to become journalists? A career press officer will never anchor the network nightly news or write a nationally syndicated column, and I met no press officers with that combination of analytical ability, writing skill, and overdrive that is apparent in the best reporters. Still, the good press officers I studied in 1981–82 were at least on an intellectual par with most of the Washington reporters I studied in 1977–78, perhaps comparable in quality to an older wire service reporter at all save the most prestigious beats. Nor will the career press officer become chief of naval operations or ambassador to Great Britain, but not many others will either. And unlike many in government's elite corps, I found that most press officers I interviewed were satisfied with the usefulness of what they were doing; several were disarmingly idealistic about their work. "I'm here to help the public get as much information as I can," said a lieutenant colonel with intensity. And a young man at the FDA, embarrassed, commented, "I've a feeling I'm doing some good. I don't have to lie to myself."

IF ACCESS is the prime quality that reporters look for in press secretaries, it is responsiveness that they want from career press officers. Responsiveness is measured by the speed with which requested information is delivered. A reporter snaps, "The army is useless. Quote me." The person he is trying to reach is at a Christmas party. An hour later, much subdued, he says, "I finally got my source." Another reporter has been waiting for some information "on a simple matter relating to a Titan launch " for two hours. He is nearing deadline. At that moment he thinks "the navy people are total losers."

When press officers are asked what qualities are most useful in their work, they mention stamina, curiosity, a helpful nature, a good memory, civility, coolness under pressure, and an understanding of human psychology. As I watched them at work I came to agree that these are attributes that distinguish good ones from the pack. The better the press officer, the more business he attracts, the longer the hours he works. The sequence can be read in either direction. A press officer says that when reporters found he was at the office until seven or eight each night, they would keep calling him. Richard Cattani of the *Christian Science Monitor* commented, "Who you can reach determines what you use. A journalism review article could be devoted to 'sourcing and metabolism.'"

Like the press secretaries they serve, career press officers need not be experts in the fields their agency covers. A manager of press officers at the Pentagon said, "I have professionals, not experts. There's not an expert in this room." Across the hall in the pressroom, one of the younger reporters noted that public affairs is "a specialty without skills. What special talents do they need?" The technical skills of the press officer, it is true, would hardly qualify for professional standing: they set up press conferences and interviews, write and distribute news releases, service the equipment needs of print and electronic journalists, arrange transportation and hotel accommodations for traveling reporters, issue press credentials, prepare news summaries and digests, copyedit transcripts of briefings. These are relatively simple matters to master, as is evident from the fact that even at the White House, government's most politically sensitive location, press logistics are extraordinarily well handled by the most junior members of the staff, people who are almost always without journalism experience; the same functions at the State Department are performed by employees who tend to have come up through the secretarial/clerical ranks. A Foreign Service officer says, "these skills are not so arcane that it is necessary to get a masters in communication from some second-rate institution."

Some skills are about as professional in character as journalism is a profession. These are the aspects of the press officer's job that could be categorized as predictive. Here a skill is not in knowing how to arrange the logistics of a press conference but in being able to predict what questions the reporters are likely to ask. Similarly, a good press officer knows how a story will be played in newspapers and on TV, what the press's reaction will be to alternative responses, what the consequences will be of not responding, and which reporters will cause problems. A failure to make the correct prediction is recounted by a former FDA attorney:

> Surprising as it may now seem [1981], one of the Food and Drug Administration's main concerns was that its announcement about saccharin's cancer-causing properties might panic consumers. Accordingly, the agency's statement [1977] repeated language from the Canadian press release, which emphasized the high doses that the test animals had been fed. Ironically, this emphasis on the relative dose levels—the agency stated that a person would have to drink 800 cans of soft drinks to consume the amount of saccharin that had been fed to the rats in the Canadian study—seriously weakened the credibility of the agency's basic conclusion, which was that saccharin could no longer be considered safe for humans.[31]

On the other hand, in 1979 when federal agencies were under attack after the near-disaster at Three Mile Island, congressional committee members had praise for the FDA because they had read a story that had been inspired by that agency's press office:

> It was late last Saturday night, and an Air Force C-130 jet transport was revving its engines on the windswept runway at Scott Air Force Base in Belleville, Ill. Soon it had loaded an unusual chemical cargo, concocted hastily at a nearby laboratory, and was air-borne for Harrisburg, Pa.
>
> The jet played a little-known, but potentially crucial, role in the unfolding Pennsylvania nuclear drama. For it carried thousands of little bottles of potassium iodide, to be taken, two drops a day, by every resident of the area near the stricken Three Mile Island nuclear plant in case of a major dispersion of radioactive material to avoid cancer of the thyroid gland.
>
> Through the breakneck efforts of the Food and Drug Administration, 259,000 bottles of the medicine are on hand today.[32]

Prediction in Washington is made easier because reporters and officials read and listen to the same media. Knowing that each morning reporters will be studying the *New York Times* and the *Washington Post* adds to the probability that a story appearing in these papers, particularly if it is on the front page, will be the subject of a question at White House, State Department, and Pentagon briefings. Alan Romberg, deputy spokesman at the State Department, was told by his predecessor that it would be possible to predict 80 percent of the questions asked each day and says that he has found this estimate correct. Many of the other 20 percent—the off-the-wall questions— come from reporters who work for marginal news organizations and therefore can be more easily deflected, as in these responses from a White House briefing: "You know I am not going to address a foolish question" and "Really, Laura, that's just nonsense."

The most important and the least understood role of the press officer, however, is that of being a connecting link between reporters and the bureaucracy. If they were to be invited to view press operations from the inside, many reporters would be surprised to see the extent to which the press officer is their advocate within the permanent government. This is even true at the State Department where, of the five agencies I observed, the press office functions least as a reporter's ombudsman. A young State Department press officer is trying to get a reporter some data on Argentina's trade with the Soviet Union. "Look," she says into the phone, "you tell me what it's proper for me to tell him, but I must have the information to do *my* job." She does not get the information. The reporter thinks that the press office is conspiring against him.

Reporters do not think of press officers as their insiders because this would imply equality, and the workplace camaraderie between reporters and press officers does not reflect the lighthearted touch of equals. Rather, putting aside whatever sexism may be involved in some cases, reporters joke with career press officers in the same way that some executives joke with other people's secretaries, a banter based on a secure knowledge that one is of higher rank and therefore it is tacky to flaunt it. This inequality was least apparent at the Pentagon where, I think, the difference was that twenty-five of the thirty-nine regular reporters had served in the armed forces; in a sense they were once part of that bureaucracy themselves.[33]

The role of the press officer as the reporters' link to government is often a much more difficult assignment at the bottom than at the top. High officials, such as members of a president's cabinet, have their own reasons for wanting to keep their names in view. Some tolerate reporters' questions as a protection against their enemies;[34] others, particularly those who have been members of Congress, genuinely enjoy the company of reporters. But in the bureaucracy, reporters are considered either frightening or unalloyed nuisances: they are snoopers, troublemakers; publicity is the enemy of sound public administration; reporters do not understand complicated programs or technical jargon; they misquote or quote out of context. The deeper that reporters wander into the bureaucracy, the more likely it is that they will be greeted with suspicion. Partly it is a matter of familiarity. Those who work for trade and specialized publications say they have no trouble getting information once they have established their bona fides. "We slowly, painstakingly, build up an aura of trust," says Louis Rothschild, editor of *Food Chemical News*, who spends every Tuesday walking the corridors of the FDA's Parklawn building in Rockville, Maryland. But bureaucrats do not often get called on by people from NBC or *Newsweek*, and they are not much in the habit of opening the door to strangers. Moreover, these strangers ask a different kind of question. Unlike the specialized reporter, they are most interested in politics, the politics of a decision or a program or an appointment. So the farther these reporters wander from the political level of government, the less authority a worker has to respond to their questions.

The bureaucracy appears equally strange and frustrating to generalist reporters, still the majority in Washington. As government grows, its parts are increasingly hidden and hard to find. Its workers cannot say things in plain English. They talk bafflegab. Bureaucrats are also ignorant of the rules that have been painfully developed in the reporter/politician relationship. "At the end of a twenty-minute conversation they will say, 'But, of course, you're not going to quote me,'" remarks an exasperated reporter used to dealing with political figures who understand that the ground rules of attribution are established at the outset of an interview.[35]

Enter the government press officer. How would you describe your job? "I'm a legman for working reporters," says Edward Nida, a senior press officer at the FDA. Increasingly the press officer gathers information from the bureaucracy that reporters request. To the degree that these career personnel, although not specialists, are more specialists than most reporters, the system promotes accuracy: there is less chance that information will be garbled. The press officer translates the language of the government's experts for the reporter.

But while press officers may be more expert than reporters, to the expert they are not experts. (The exception, of course, is the military press officer when his account is his branch of the armed forces.) The press officer looks like a bureaucrat to the reporter and like a reporter to the bureaucrat. Bill Rados, a career press officer, comments that at an FDA meeting, for instance, someone will make a disparaging remark about reporters, then in embarrassment quickly add, "present company excepted." Thus the insiders see press officers as outsiders, and, to some extent, this is the way press officers see themselves. As an illustration of this perception, consider that no government official who thinks of himself exclusively as a government official would argue that the press should be privy to internal policy deliberations. Yet in 1979 when twelve career press officers at the Department of Health, Education, and Welfare were asked whether they believed HEW public information officers should disclose information on policy deliberations within their agency, seven said "yes" and three refused to answer.[36] That sentiment should also startle reporters, who have felt themselves at times in a tug-of-war with press officers.

A portrait of the career press officer emerges: semibureaucrat/semireporter, in the bureaucracy but not truly of it, tainted by association with the press yet not of the press. They are individually more competent than the reputation of their occupation, at least at the agencies I examined. They are not usually in a position within the government to manipulate more than the most routine information, even if they would want to. And just as the political press secretary is often suspect in the eyes of the political executive, so too the career press officer is often the odd person out in the permanent bureaucracy.

CHAPTER 4

Routine Activities

IF PRESS OFFICERS kept daily time sheets, most of what they do could be charged to four types of activities: informing themselves and their colleagues, preparing material for the news media, staging events, and responding to reporters' inquiries. Preparing material for the press and staging events can be considered assertive activities—the government's effort to set its imprint on the shape of the news. Responding to reporters' inquiries, on the other hand, is largely reactive. The other activities are in the nature of organizational maintenance and are not directly related to press relations. Looking at these routines individually and then trying to assess the time spent on each is one way of addressing the concern that press operations may have become more manipulative than is appropriate in a democratic society.

PRESS OFFICERS must try to keep themselves up-to-date on what reporters think they should know about their agencies' activities. To a considerable degree they do this by cadging information as best they can: they are, after all, outsiders within the bureaucracy. Indeed, some of their information will come from reporters. Listening to telephone conversations of a particularly talented press officer, I was sometimes left with the impression that she had asked more questions than the reporter (*you may know more about that than I do . . .*) and that the reporter had done most of the talking.

Other information will come from nonsystematic reading. The State Department press office, for example, keeps a reading file, a folder of memos, cables, and clippings that press officers are expected to peruse whenever they have spare time. There were twenty-five items in the file on May 20, 1982, including situation report 59 of the Falklands Working Group and situation report 174 of the Poland Working Group; two research papers, "China's Relations in South Asia" and "Liberia—The Political Outlook Through 1985"; various cables from overseas posts with such titles as "Another Case of Abuse of U.S. Journalists" (confidential) and "Zaire Decision to Reject U.S. Aid" (secret); some official documents, such as the "Final Communiqué of NATO Foreign Ministers' Meeting in Luxembourg"; an editorial from the *Jerusalem Post* stamped for "limited official use"; and an assortment of memos, among them, "A Revised Speech Strategy" (for Secretary of State Alexander Haig) and "A Proposed Media Program" (for White House Chief of Staff James Baker). It was a useful miscellany of items, none of which would have surprised a careful reader of the *New York Times*.

The formal route for internal information within a government agency is for it to be passed along from meeting to meeting. At the State and Defense departments the chain starts with a daily early morning session held by the secretary. A regular participant describes a typical secretary's meeting at the Pentagon in 1981:

> 8:30 a.m. Lasts half-hour/forty-five minutes. Fifteen principals (deputy secretary, under secretaries, assistant secretaries) plus small group of spear carriers, military assistants. Weinberger leads off: talks about principal issues, what president is interested in, top visitors of the day, budget questions. Asks around table in order of rank. [Deputy Secretary] Carlucci will have quite a lot to say; he's very much the manager of the building. Next biggest discussion will be about legislation. Public affairs may talk about what's coming up in terms of interviews that day. Weinberger gives quick guidance. Perhaps he will want us to set up backgrounder. He will have read all the clips (gets up at 5:30); may have mild objections to one or two stories. Often just getting it out of his system; not necessarily cue to us to call the reporters.

Such meetings, which the innermost circle find tedious, are particularly valuable for those with more limited access. Alert press officers use the moments before and after the meetings to talk informally with the other officials. An FDA veteran notes, "I'll go up to the commissioner and ask, 'Doctor, can I have two minutes?'" A Pentagon press officer adds, "These fill-ins are important for us. These people are too busy to call public affairs. You have to find out yourself. There's no time to cross-fertilize."

The FDA commissioner meets weekly with his policy board; then the associate commissioner for public affairs meets with the three units that report to him, the principal agenda item being a debriefing on the commissioner's meeting. Finally, the press office support staff (three full-time secretaries and a part-timer) meet "so they will know what each press officer is working on and will know to whom to refer calls." It is a process that most taxes those in the middle, who must attend meetings to receive information and then meetings to transmit that information.

At the White House Edwin Meese, James Baker, and Michael Deaver meet daily at 7:30 a.m.; senior staff meet at 8:30; and Press Secretary Larry Speakes's staff meets at 8:45 (twelve to fifteen attending, including a representative from Mrs. Reagan and Vice President Bush). The press secretary first reviews the president's schedule, annotated for photo opportunities and backgrounders. He continues with notes from the earlier meetings, indicating points and activities to be emphasized. Junior staff members then provide oral summaries of the major morning newspapers. Finally, Speakes gives a few assignments or directives: instructions on how to handle a Rose Garden ceremony—"tight toe lines" (participants should be grouped close together). "Who wants to cover a Meese speech at noon and report back to me?" "The Consumer Price Index is being released today. What was the figure when the administration took office?"

Whether they are held in the west wing of the White House or in a fifteenth-floor conference room at FDA headquarters off Rockville Pike, meetings serve the same purpose: they pass along the information necessary to lubricate the system. But there is always a potential hazard in distributing information this way. "It's like the old game that kids play," says a State Department spokesman in a somewhat different context. "You whisper in somebody's ear and pass it down through ten people. By the time it gets to the tenth person it's distorted. It's not a deliberate attempt on anybody's part to distort anything. It just sometimes happens."

These meetings also hold out the possibility that the press might acquire inside information. The possibility increases in direct proportion to the length of time an administration is in office as internal policy struggles harden into personal feuds and as reporters get to know officials. The leaks become increasingly embarrassing to the administration as the next election approaches. What then happens is predictable. "The bigger the meeting, the less useful," says a former State Department spokesman. Meetings start to shrink and are held less frequently. "I used to have a weekly meeting," one Transportation Department official comments, "but it became obvious that they didn't want to air their problems before each other." "Daily meetings became burdensome," says a Pentagon official who has more important tasks than keeping the chain of information intact. He sends his assistant to represent him. Soon other officials, seeing that they are meeting with assistants, start to send their assistants.

There is also more caution about what is committed to paper. At the secretary of transportation's senior staff meeting (twenty-three principals, four spear carriers) an administrator warns that tightly scheduled deadlines will make a program look like a failure if the document gets into the hands of the press. Another administrator agrees that there is no need for "lots of paper." A third jokes, "we leaked the second draft, not the first." The laughter is restrained. Political executives become less willing to keep their organizations informed.

EARLY on weekday mornings most public affairs offices in the government read, clip, duplicate, and circulate news stories. It is the press officers' way of informing their bosses and themselves of what items reported in the news will directly or indirectly affect their operations. The compilation is called *Current News* at the Department of Defense, *News Digest* at the Department of Transportation, *News Today* at the Arms Control and Disarmament Agency, and *News Roundup* at the State Department's Bureau of Inter-American Affairs. The White House prefers to summarize the news so that what it distributes is more like a compilation of lead paragraphs. *

Which employees are considered of sufficient importance to receive this service, at what time, and in what form, is a matter of some status. At the White House a first printing of 125 copies is available at 6:00 a.m. at the southwest gate, where they are picked up by the chauffeurs of cabinet members and the most exalted presidential advisers. Lesser members of the White House staff must wait until 9:00 a.m. when another 300 copies are distributed. The first edition of DOT's news clips goes to 15 executives—a later version goes to 180—but only 3 get their copies with key paragraphs underlined for them in yellow, a subtle suggestion that their reading time is just a bit more valuable. The Federal Highway Administration distributes 27 copies of its daily clips and the Department of Defense distributes 5,000.

Circulation and readership are not the same, of course. The news clips are often duplicated within a unit or simply passed down the chain of command. The FDA's *Daily Clipping Service* has a circulation of 50, but a 1981 survey showed that each copy was seen by 14 people. Most government executives learn what is being written about them, their agencies, and their enemies through these internal compendiums.

Moreover, the closer government officials are to the top, the less likely they are to be casual consumers of news and the more likely to have their news prepackaged for them. This has consequences. The officials experience the product of journalism in a far more intensive form than the rest of us. We may read parts of a daily newspaper, sections of a weekly newsmagazine, and watch some news on television; they are exposed to massive and regular dosages of news on limited subjects. The officials may come to believe that journalists are more influential in shaping public opinion than they actually

* See "Documents," pp. 122–25.

are. For example, on Thursday, January 7, 1982, a not very exciting day for transportation news, DOT's *News Digest* was thirty-six pages. Such a steady diet of news clips can lead, as scholar Leon Sigal suggested to me, to a "sort of pluralistic ignorance—a reinforced preoccupation with the importance of what an official is doing."

Most Americans say their news comes from television, but the daily clips, the news staple of government officials, are a collection of newspaper and magazine articles. This, too, has consequences. While it would be possible to include a transcript of TV news, transcripts are expensive to produce and are not a regular feature at most agencies. Nor do transcripts (at the Pentagon) or summaries (at the White House) adequately reflect what appears on television, where the reporter's words are only one element of the story. The White House Communications Agency prepares a composite tape of the three networks' evening news programs, which usually runs slightly over thirty minutes and can be seen on sets in the White House offices at 9:30 a.m. and 12:30 p.m. This special channel also replays the weekend talk shows. The audience is probably not large; most presidential assistants have more pressing obligations in the middle of the day. Such broadcasting, however, has symbolic significance: the president's staff understand the importance of network television in nationalizing impressions—even if it is not the way they get their own information. But throughout the rest of government, the daily clipping services provide additional evidence that the news rhythm of official Washington is determined by the print media, notably certain newspapers.

A survey shows that 45 percent of high federal officials regularly read the *New York Times*.[1] More important, all high government officials know what the *New York Times* is writing about them and their immediate concerns. And if they miss something in their daily clips, they learn about it through word-of-mouth. The same is true of the *Washington Post*, a hometown paper for government workers. On January 26, 1982, the *Post's* Mike Causey wrote, "The Department of Transportation yesterday gave out RIF (layoff) notices to 237 of its 1,100 staffers at the Office of the Secretary here." Causey's column was reproduced that day in the clips of DOT's Office of Public Affairs, the Urban Mass Transportation Administration, the Federal Highway Administration, the Federal Railroad Administration, and the National Highway Traffic Safety Administration. There may be DOT employees who do not get home delivery or do not buy a paper on the way to work—or who are inattentive readers—but duplicating machines and corridor conversation make it almost impossible to be unaware of a major item about the department that appears in the *Post*.

In fifteen editions of daily clips at the Arms Control and Disarmament Agency, randomly selected over three months, 254 articles were reprinted: two-thirds of those items came from the *Times* or the *Post* (43 percent *Times*; 26 percent *Post*). Thirteen other publications combined to provide the remaining 31 percent. The institution of the daily clips thus magnifies the influence of the *New York Times* and the *Washington Post*, just as it diminishes the influence of ABC, CBS, and NBC.

Other newspapers that make the early editions of the daily clips—the ones in the cars that pick up cabinet officials at their homes—are often determined by when they arrive at the agencies. The Baltimore *Sun* and the *Philadelphia Inquirer* are well positioned; the importance of location is further illustrated by the fact that the *Washington Times*, founded in 1982 by the Reverend Sun Myung Moon's Unification Church, instantly turned up in some key agencies' daily clips. The *Los Angeles Times*, on the other hand, is an outstanding newspaper that unfortunately cannot fly copies across country in time to be read by the secretaries of state and defense on their way to work. According to its diplomatic correspondent, Oswald Johnston, the organization "tried everything—short of buying an airline—to get papers to Washington early enough to be included in the a.m. clips, including routing papers to arrive at National [the close-in Washington airport]. But this meant changing planes in Chicago, which often caused delays. So the papers now come in on the 'red eye' that arrives at Dulles about 7:30, and, with off-loading and ground transportation, they don't get to the office until 9:30." This problem, however, will be solved by the use of computers. Indeed, by mid-1982 the White House already subscribed to a computerized service that summarized the day's stories from selected newspapers around the country, including some on the West Coast. Eventually, then, the daily clips will become the daily printouts, and access to a publication will no longer be limited by its location.

In his book on the Nixon administration, William Safire reproduces a copy of a White House news summary on which the president has written, "Good job, Ron," meaning that he wished to send a congratulatory letter to Governor Ronald Reagan, and "K— we must get *all hands* in line on this," meaning that he wanted National Security Adviser Henry Kissinger to follow up.[2] Thus the daily clips and news summaries are also used as a vehicle for sending messages to supporters and staff members. At the lower level at which I observed government, I often found that the bosses' marginal notes were instructions to their press officers to prepare a letter to the editor or request a correction on an offending story.

Although produced by government agencies for government agencies, the clipping services I examined during 1981–82 closely followed the tenets of American journalism. The material was arranged in order of importance (top story on the front page) and did not downplay bad news. One government editor did admit, however, that he might bump an unfavorable piece about his boss from page 1 to page 2, and Bill Hart, who heads the four-person news summary operation for President Reagan, says he never includes stories about alleged staff feuds (instead he sends the articles to the individuals involved). But generally I found the government's daily clips provided an accurate reflection of how the commercial media were playing the news. Eighteen editions of *The White House News Summary*, chosen at random over four months, showed no weighting in favor of those writers whose views coincided with President Reagan's. Syndicated columnists noted for pronounced political ideologies, such as Tom Wicker or William F. Buckley, were given balanced treatment. There were twenty-two summaries of seven liberals and nineteen summaries of six conservatives. Nor was the president spared from the wrath of newspaper editorialists. The following item, in its entirety, is the summary of a *New York Times* editorial on September 18, 1981:

THE PROMISE OF AWACS

The sale should never have been proposed, no less promised. President Reagan would be wise to retreat before he is frontally defeated.

There were marginal differences between the daily clips in the different agencies. The White House puts a premium on being representative; my sample had editorials from twenty papers, including the *Anchorage Daily News*. Because the Transportation secretary had been a Pennsylvania politician, the person in charge of DOT's press clips, like any wise editor, kept his primary audience's interests in mind. Those who prepared the Food and Drug Administration's press clips seemed to want their service to be educational in that articles often did not directly relate to the agency: on October 13, 1981, for instance, only seven of thirty-three items even mentioned the FDA by name.

The most elaborate and respected government clipping service comes from the Pentagon. Under the direction of Harry Zubkoff, chief of the News Clipping and Analysis Service, and his top editor, Helen Young, seven persons working two shifts review 45 newspapers and more than 120 magazines. *Current News* comes in two sections: an early bird edition at 7:30 a.m. deals with breaking events; a second part arrives at 11:30 a.m. and features editorials, columns, and articles from the hinterland. Radio-TV transcripts are provided by a private company. Frequent special editions are devoted to a single topic, such as a major military exercise. "This is one frill that Congress never questions. Both supporters and opponents [of the military] find it too useful," says a colonel. Richard Gross, UPI's Pentagon correspondent, told me, "yesterday I said to this guy, 'I see your story made an inside page.' He replied, 'Yes, but it was page 1 in the publication that really counts around here.'"

To paraphrase what used to be the slogan of the *Philadelphia Bulletin*, at the Defense Department nearly everybody reads the daily clips. Richard Halloran of the *New York Times*, notes that "the clips make it a whole lot easier to operate around here because a whole lot of people get to know your name a lot faster than they would otherwise. Look at Charlie Corddry. He's very respected. He works for the Baltimore *Sun*. How many people would read Charlie if it weren't for this?" A consequence from the vantage point of sources—the officials to whom reporters go seeking information—is that they thus have the knowledge with which to assess a reporter's intelligence and reliability. The consequence from the vantage point of reporters is that they may get their calls answered without having to be from the elite press. Strangely, then, while the daily clips at most agencies serve to increase the influence of the *Times* and *Post*, at the Pentagon the daily clips act as a great equalizer among reporters.[3]

The State Department does not have a clipping service at the departmental level; the various subunits do their own clipping. State also discontinued keeping a daily transcript of network TV news during the Carter administration. Thomas Reston, then deputy assistant secretary for public affairs, polled the seventh floor—the secretary's office—and found that very few people were reading it. So he stopped the transcript as a cost-cutting measure. His decision had no hidden political motive in the opinion of the press corps. Some TV reporters complained, however; they wanted the top diplomats to know what they were saying about them.

ANOTHER major activity of press offices is to prepare information for the news media—the ubiquitous press release.* A young reporter at the *Washington Post's* "Federal Report" page has the additional responsibility of sorting news releases that come in every day. He raises a hand to illustrate that the daily pile is about a foot high: "The agencies are abusing the use of paper."

That government press offices produce a blizzard of releases is hardly in dispute. In 1981 the Defense Department's Public Affairs Office issued 585

*See "Documents," pp. 126–29.

"blue tops" (the in-house name for its handouts). The State Department was slightly less prolific, issuing 441 news releases; in the same period, its New York office at the United Nations turned out at least 160 additional releases. Neither the State Department nor the Pentagon, however, is in a class with the White House. I counted 14 handouts in the newsroom rack on a June day in 1982. These included the president's schedule for the day, the president's revised schedule, a list of those who would be attending the swearing-in ceremony in the Rose Garden for the new chairman of the Joint Chiefs of Staff, a biography of the new chairman of the Joint Chiefs of Staff, the president's remarks at the swearing-in of the chairman of the Joint Chiefs of Staff, announcements of two White House staff appointments (one a special assistant to the president to help "identify and correct state laws which discriminate against women"), announcements that bills would be signed to designate National Inventors Day and to give a name to the air traffic control tower at Memphis International Airport, a list of members of the House of Representatives who would be meeting with the president to discuss the budget, a packet of material from Mrs. Reagan's office about a luncheon she was giving for wives of present and former U.S. senators, a message from the president to the Congress urging favorable consideration of a fishery agreement between the United States and Poland, and the transcript of remarks made from the south lawn by Prime Minister Menachem Begin of Israel.

To read hundreds of government releases—as I did in 1981–82—is not a stimulating experience. During December 1981 the Department of Transportation turned out eighteen (and three texts of congressional testimony), but only two could be considered of general newsworthiness: the administration's proposals on maritime regulatory reform and a statement by DOT Secretary Drew Lewis reopening federal employment, other than at the FAA, to the air traffic controllers who had been dismissed as a result of the strike against the government. As with most of the releases produced by government, DOT's December output was mainly intended for specific audiences, such as a locality or an industry: a program to test new buses in Providence, El Paso, Columbus, and Lansing; the sale of 93.4 miles of Conrail lines in Massachusetts and Connecticut. Only one release struck me as being without merit as written ("Coast Guard to Simplify Paperwork Procedures").

What becomes clear is that most government releases are simply brief recitations of some facts about an event. At the Pentagon, a typical release (477-81) begins, "North Pole Refining Co., North Pole, Alaska, was awarded on December 16, 1981, a $31,968,702.00 fixed price with escalation contract for JP-4 fuel, following competition in which 188 bids were solicited and 59 were received." Awards of all contracts over $3 million are regularly listed in a handout, but with escalating inflation the department is thinking of pushing up the minimum for an announcement to $5 million. These releases are issued only after the stock market closes for the day. Another common topic of Pentagon releases is the commissioning of ships, as in 490-81:

> The Department of the Navy announced today that OHIO (SSBN-726), first of a new class of nuclear powered ballistic missile submarines, will be commissioned at 11:00 a.m., November 11. . . . OHIO class submarines are 560 feet long, have a beam of 42 feet and displace 18,700 tons when submerged. OHIO will initially carry 24 TRIDENT-1 (C-4) missiles as compared to the 16 POSEIDON or TRIDENT-1 missiles carried by today's ballistic missile submarines. OHIO class submarines will eventually carry 24 TRIDENT-II (D-5) missiles, an evolutionary follow-on anticipated to be operational in 1989.

Press releases can be difficult to produce. At the FDA, for instance, a problem in writing releases is often how to explain scientific information to a lay audience. "It's a continuing source of tension between my office and the people who are working with the subject we are writing about," said press chief Wayne Pines. Also, because FDA releases can become evidence in a court of law, each must go through an elaborate prepublication process: three writing stages (initial drafting, technical editing, copy editing), five internal clearance steps, and more perfunctory approval from the press offices at the Public Health Service and the Department of Health and Human Services. Clearances can take two to three weeks, a source of frustration to public information officers who have come from employment in news organizations or congressional offices.

The releases are helpful to nonspecialist reporters. "Paracoccidioidomycosis," explains FDA release P81-11, is "a serious and sometimes fatal chronic disease of the lungs. Also known as South American blastomycosis, it is commonly found in Central and South America." P82-1 notes that "angina is pronounced an-JI-nah, or the Latin pronunciation, AN-je-nah" and "Nifedipine is pronounced ni-FED-a-peen"—a bit of advice that would be of use to broadcasters. Some regulatory agencies, however, are notorious for making sure their jargon cannot be deciphered without fraternal initiation. One generalist reporter said, "you need a degree in nuclear physics to understand NRC [Nuclear Regulatory Commission] releases."

Government releases can be useful and accurate and still be incomplete and even deceptive because they are an agency's opportunity to order information in a manner that the agency considers most advantageous to its mission. The FDA, for instance, put out a sixteen-paragraph news release (P81-12) announcing approval of aspartame, a low-calorie sweetener. Given the 1970 banning of cyclamate and the subsequent saccharin controversy, this was a decision of some note. The next-to-last paragraph of the release observed that the commissioner had overruled a scientific public board of inquiry, chaired by a professor from the Massachusetts Institute of Technology, which had recommended "aspartame not be approved until further long-term animal testing could be conducted." But when *American Pharmacy* reported "FDA Approves Aspartame" in an eighteen-paragraph article in October 1981, its second paragraph was devoted to the board of inquiry's recommendation. News release and article contained the same facts; their emphases, however, were markedly different.

When the Federal Aviation Administration announced in January 1982 a twenty-year plan for updating and modernizing the nation's air traffic control and air navigation system, the news release (FAA 02-82) and fact sheet seemed to be installments in "The Case of the Missing Facts." Neither included figures on the proposal's cost or on how it was to be paid for. This might have been an oversight had the government's material not repeatedly referred to cost savings. At a time when President Reagan was stressing budget and tax restraint, FAA administrator J. Lynn Helms apparently thought he could distract reporters with an announcement that, according to the *Journal of Commerce*, "concentrated on the technical marvels to come."[4] But readers of the next day's newspapers learned what readers of the FAA's handouts would not have known: the proposed new system was estimated to cost $9 billion and would be paid for, Congress willing, by additional taxes on airline tickets and the fuel used by jet and piston-driven planes.

Releases were most often sneered at by those reporters whose claim to status was based largely on their belief that journalists are by definition superior to government "flacks." But such reactions may reflect the concerns of the reporters more accurately than the inadequacies of government handouts. The handouts, according to one observer, may be "often underrated by reporters who are unwilling to admit their dependence on them."[5] After experiencing various aspects of the government's public information bureaucracy, I came to agree with *Washington Post* reporter Felicity Barringer, who had told me I would find that "releases are readable and competent. There is not much frivolous stuff about little Johnny Jones."[6] Stylistically, they were at least on a par with routine wire service copy. "There's an art to it," said the FDA's Jim Greene, pointing to two inches of documents on sodium that he had compressed into a draft release of less than three pages.

ON SEPTEMBER 30, 1981, the Food and Drug Administration held a public hearing on "patient package insert," a proposal requiring that prescription drugs be sold with a brochure that states, in simple language, the drug's purpose, side effects, and proper use.

On January 28, 1982, the Federal Aviation Administration briefed reporters and industry representatives on a 450-page report that proposed extensive modernization of the nation's air traffic control and air navigation system.

On March 22, 1982, the State Department released "Chemical Warfare in Southeast Asia and Afghanistan," a document that was introduced to reporters by the deputy secretary and then explained by a panel of five experts.

These three events were staged by the government in large part so that they would be reported in the press. Similar events take place every day in Washington. Reporters are alerted through news releases, items on the wire services' day book, and phone calls. Arrangements have to be made to handle the special logistical needs of broadcasters. Fact sheets are prepared to highlight, summarize, or simplify the issues from the government's standpoint. Transcripts and sometimes even videotapes are made available. Press officers must consider how to make these events as interesting and attractive as possible. Who should be the presenters? What should be the order of witnesses? Should graphs and other visual materials be used? In some cases it is necessary to draft remarks for the participants and to hold rehearsals. The event is competing with other events staged by other organizations and will receive the attention that editors or producers think it deserves. The air control system proposal, for example, was reported the next day on page 1 of the *New York Times*, page 2 of the *Journal of Commerce*, page 3 of the *Wall Street Journal*, page 4 of the *Philadelphia Inquirer*, and page 17 of the *Washington Post*.

Although collectively the executive branch is a movable feast for Washington reporters, the typical government agency initiates very few events, especially when compared with the daily menu of congressional hearings.[7] For instance, there are just two or three public hearings at the FDA in a year. During the three months I spent at the State Department, the only large-scale briefing comparable to the one on chemical warfare took place when Secretary Haig reported on his attempts to negotiate the Falklands dispute. There is one significant exception to the modest behavior, however: the White House is expected to put on a daily show.

Reporting on presidents is almost entirely a matter of reporting events. In part this reflects the reality of what presidents do. Much of their attention is devoted to symbolic roles that require being publicly noticed. As head of state they greet other heads of state; as chief politician they endorse the candidates of their party; as head of the executive branch they must be seen negotiating with the heads of the legislative branch; as chief manager of the government they must be seen meeting with or instructing their lieutenants. Journalists complain bitterly about being used as props in these activities, but staging events also reflects the limitations of reality. The growth of the White House press corps and the need to be concerned about presidential security combine to confine a large number of reporters, photographers, and technicians and a great deal of equipment in two small newsrooms and a forty-eight-seat briefing room. In the absence of interviews and personal confidences that reporters expect from senators or governors, the president's press staff offers a steady stream of events and photo opportunities that at least serve as a release valve on the pressure cooker that is the White House beat. On a Tuesday in June 1982, a not exceptionally busy day by White House standards, the press office provided the following activities for the amusement and edification of the regulars on the beat:

> Larry Speakes' first briefing for reporters at 9:15 in his office; an opportunity to take pictures and eavesdrop on a few minutes of a session between President Reagan and Republican congressional leaders in the Cabinet Room (9:30); a mid-morning briefing by an assistant secretary of state on the president's meeting with President Monge of Costa Rica; the press secretary's usual noon briefing; a mid-afternoon briefing by an Education Department official on the president's tuition tax credit proposal; a chance to interview two senators who have failed to talk the president out of vetoing a housing bill; and in late afternoon the last opportunity of the day to take a picture of the president, this time shaking hands with congressional candidates and their spouses.

While the briefings are off limits to television cameras, TV clearly dominates the thinking and planning of the White House press office. The beat now focuses on one story a day because the networks are not going to use more than one major White House story on their nightly news program. Thus the contest between the press office and the pressroom is largely over what event will rise to the top each day. This tug-of-war is illustrated by two events of June 23, 1982:

—Buses take the White House reporters to CIA headquarters in Langley, Virginia, for the signing of the Intelligence Identities Protection Act of 1982. It is not a major piece of legislation. The ceremony is designed so that the president can pay tribute to those government employees of "the shadowy world" who "must serve in silence." The weather is beautiful. The setting is impressive. Mr. Reagan tells a funny story.

—British Prime Minister Margaret Thatcher meets President Reagan in late afternoon. The Falklands' fighting has just ended. The White House wants to rebuild damaged relations in Latin America and would prefer to downplay the Thatcher visit. The meeting concludes at an inconvenient time for television reporters, minutes before the network news goes on the air.

That evening ABC devoted 20 seconds to the CIA story and 120 seconds to the Thatcher story; on CBS, it was 20 seconds and 180 seconds; NBC ran the Thatcher story for 100 seconds and did not use the CIA story.[8] The story and a photograph of Reagan and Thatcher were on the front page of the *Washington Post*, which put the CIA story and a photograph on page 3. For reporters, "real" news always takes precedence over "manufactured" news. But the White House press office can be philosophical about it all. Larry Speakes tells reporters, "You don't tell us how to stage the news and we don't tell you how to cover it."

There are days when neither the news media nor the president makes the decision on the top story and other days when the president and the press pick the same event. It is not a closed system: both president and White House reporters must also respond to events initiated by Congress, the judiciary, the opposition party, other nations, and, on occasion, enterprising reporters.

THE FINAL major responsibility of press officers is to respond to reporters' inquiries. Except for the handful of government agencies that have newsrooms on the premises, press officers mainly meet reporters over the phone. Increasingly they give information to members of the press whom they do not know, will never see, and may never hear from again. Thus most of the business between government and the press is conducted as an act of faith, an assumption that people are who they say they are and that information will be accurately reported.[9]

Press officers do not tape their conversations with reporters, and rarely do they even keep a log of phone calls. However, for a week in 1981, Faye Peterson, a press officer at the FDA, agreed to keep track of her incoming calls for this study. Peterson has worked for the government since she graduated from college in 1960. She does not have a background in journalism. She reminded me of a helpful reference librarian. When a reporter called, she either had the information at her fingertips, looked it up, or referred the inquirer to the appropriate expert. In that week, she answered seventeen requests for information:

—*Diet pills*, including a story that a woman had died after taking a weight control drug: four calls—National Public Radio, TV stations in Washington and Kansas City, and an unspecified Canadian publication.

—*Bendectin*, a drug prescribed for morning sickness that has been the subject of birth defect lawsuits: three calls—"The Today Show" (NBC), the *New York Times* (a reporter in New York), and an Orlando, Florida, TV station.

—*DMSO*, an industrial solvent promoted without FDA approval as a remedy for various illnesses: two calls—a Buffalo radio station and a Los Angeles TV station.

—*Gene splicing*, FDA authorization to conduct tests of a synthetic human growth hormone: two calls—UPI and a New York City TV station.

—*Patient package inserts*: one call from a free-lance writer.

—*Interferon*, a natural antivirus substance that was being tested as a possible cure for diseases ranging from cancer to the common cold: one call from the *London Times*.

—*Antibiotics*: a periodic call from *Science* magazine on the status of approvals.

—*Herpes*: one call from the Cleveland *Press*.

—*Blood banking*: one call from *Family Weekly* magazine.

—*Whooping cough vaccine*: one call from a consumer/investigative reporter for a Washington TV station, of which Peterson said, "I think I convinced her that she was barking up the wrong tree."

The pattern of Linda Gosden's telephone calls—at least those that took place during the parts of twelve days that I sat in her office—was very different. As director of public affairs for the Department of Transportation, she gave the impression of spending most of her waking hours cradling a phone receiver. When her friends gave her a surprise birthday party, the cake was decorated with a cartoon of Gosden, phone in hand, saying, "I'll put you on hold." But most of her office calls were to or from other DOT officials. Several times a day she also talked with political comrades, both in and out of government, comparing what she calls "the real skinny." I only listened to her end of nine calls from reporters, eight of whom were based in Washington. The callers were from the *New York Times* and the *Washington Post* (each paper calling twice), and single calls from the Associated Press, the *St. Louis Post-Dispatch*, ABC, CBS, and NBC. Calls from smaller news organizations tended to be taken by her special assistant, Tom Blank. As in Peterson's case, calls considered highly sensitive were bucked to the press chief.   .

Gosden had been Drew Lewis's press secretary at the Republican National

Committee; therefore, it was not surprising that four of her nine press calls were exclusively Drew Lewis stories (*Is he going to resign? Is he going to replace Ed Meese?*). Only two calls were strictly related to Department of Transportation business. Gosden's technique—if that is what it was—seemed to be to underplay a story. The opposite of the proverbial public relations type, she acted as if her capital in the National Reporters Bank was finite, so that when Lewis had a speech scheduled, for example, she would say to herself, *He isn't going to say much. How many chits should I use getting reporters there?*

LIKE ANY unit in an organization, a press office devotes part of its time to maintaining itself. And the amount of time can be considerable if, as I saw at the FDA and at DOT, there is a new administration with a strong commitment to cutting the size of government. But at any given time there is also routine maintenance that must be attended to—everything from budgeting and personnel work to scheduling training and vacations. Nonpress functions are also often attached to press offices. Executives of some subunits give enough speeches to justify hiring a full-time speechwriter, but in other cases speechwriting becomes part of some press officer's responsibilities. Then, too, press offices may prepare some material for audiences other than the press. *FDA Today*, for example, is the agency's monthly in-house newsletter.

My overall impression, however, is that press offices spend as much time responding to reporters' inquiries as they do on all other activities combined. Given that a substantial number of hours are devoted to keeping themselves informed and to pursuing internal agency business, not more than a quarter of their time is left for staging events and preparing material for the news media. The hypothetical time sheet of the press offices I observed might have the following allocation: responding to reporters' inquiries, 50 percent; keeping informed and working on agency business, 25 percent; and initiating materials and events, 25 percent. Obviously these percentages will be different for each press officer, but I observed no press officer, outside of the White House, who spent most of his time staging events or initiating material even as innocuous as handouts.

These observations suggest why most press officers I spoke with thought of their role as being largely reactive and were dubious about claims that they set the news agenda. Their opinions and my observations contradict the contentions cited in the first chapter that government press operations are mainly manipulative.

CHAPTER 5

Reactions to Crises

IT IS almost four in the afternoon, January 13, 1982, and it has been snowing hard for several hours. Government workers were told to go home some time ago, and now the city block that is the Department of Transportation building appears almost deserted. I am about to go home too, putting on my overshoes in Linda Gosden's office. We have just returned from Secretary Drew Lewis's senior staff meeting, an hour and a half devoted to a review of management priorities for the coming year. Gosden, as she does almost every day, is apologizing for taking me to a meeting that she thinks I must have found very dull. I tell her again that my study will be largely about "routine"; it is not necessary for me to observe a crisis. "Perhaps I'll still catch one at State." A young man bursts into the room. "There's a report a plane has crashed into the Fourteenth Street bridge." Gosden starts to run to Lewis's office, perhaps the length of a football field away. My unbuckled snowshoes are flapping around my ankles as I unsuccessfully try to keep up.

From the cabinet officer's windows we should be able to see the bridge that is the crash scene. We can see only the flashing red lights of emergency vehicles through the snow and darkness. Others also rush to Lewis's office. The television set is on. We keep switching channels, as people do when all stations are covering a crisis and each keeps repeating the same news. Air Florida flight 90 is down in what is apparently the worst disaster in the history of National Airport.

Gosden organizes a team to monitor the three TV networks and the wires and to relay written summaries to Lewis. All phones are in use. Lewis calls Caspar Weinberger and asks for military helicopters; the request is instantly granted. He then calls the Coast Guard commandant. He wants to know the location of the closest cutter. (It is several hours away in the lower Chesapeake Bay and will start for the site at once.) He calls the chairman of the National Transportation Safety Board, the agency responsible for determining the cause of the accident, and offers the facilities of his department, including a hangar at National Airport where the bodies can be taken. An official of Air Florida calls, and Lewis offers help in getting the plane out of the Potomac. David Gergen calls from the White House: with Gosden on an extension they compose a statement that the president might wish to make. Edwin Meese calls. He is worried that an aide may be on the plane. (Lewis's office determines that he is not.) FAA Administrator Lynn Helms is about to board a plane at Dulles Airport; Lewis directs his general counsel, John Fowler, to go to FAA headquarters and keep him informed until Helms can get there. A low-level DOT employee who happens to be on the other side of the river is dispatched to the Marriott Hotel, which the National Transportation Safety Board is using as the crash headquarters.

Eventually it is too dark and too cold to continue the rescue operation. Work is called off until morning. There are no more calls to make or answer. Bone-weary, we are reluctant to leave, to break a bond that has been created by working together through a crisis. We talk quietly. Some wonder how they will get home. Around ten o'clock, Dick Schoenfeld, Gosden's assistant, drives me to my door, and after six hours I finally take off my flapping galoshes.

Ted Cron, a former FDA press chief, once told me that the delicate balance in government press operations was to give all the information necessary to protect the public and at the same time try not to frighten people unreasonably. This had seemed to be Gosden's concern. Too many people at too many places in government could have been giving out conflicting and unsubstantiated information. Still breathless from her dash to Lewis's office, her first acts were to call the public affairs officers at the Federal Aviation Administration and National Airport, reminding them that all facts must be verified before being released. There had already been some confusion on TV about whether the plane's destination was Tampa or White Plains. The primary value of Gosden's monitoring of the media was not to learn information but to check for possible misinformation.

Gosden also had a hidden agenda. Hardly a person in Lewis's office had not initially feared the crash was a result of an air tower mistake. Lewis had been responsible for firing the striking air controllers; if lives had now been lost because of inexperienced or overworked replacements, public reaction against the Reagan administration would be swift and painful. Based on the information on visibility available to him, Lewis, a licensed pilot, concluded that air controllers were not the cause of the crash. Gosden then began a series of quick calls to the networks, whose prime-time news programs were about to go on the air. She did not rule out an error on the part of an air controller; only the National Transportation Safety Board—not an arm of

DOT—can determine the cause of an accident. Rather, Gosden gave reporters information that she hoped would allow them to draw a conclusion that the crash could not be blamed on the people in the control tower.[1]

I had seen a crisis and government's response. It was at first chaotic. Many of the people who were needed were out of contact, stuck in cars or stranded at distant places. Everyone seemed to be trying to reach the same telephone numbers. Then something special happened. Until lines of authority were sorted out, people took on tasks that were above them or beneath them. Some "important" people performed menial chores; some "unimportant" people rose to heights beyond their normal abilities or usual responsibilities. Self-protective mechanisms seemed to evaporate: No one said, "Put it in writing" or "According to the regulations. . . ." After a crisis of this kind there should be lessons to be learned, new designs for how to better anticipate and prepare, revisions of what has to be done, where, by whom, and in what order. But beyond the need for contingency planning, there is also the lesson of how well many people respond in the face of sudden adversity.

THE Air Florida tragedy was an accident, a crisis that was the result of unintentional and nongovernmental actions, yet one to which various government units, including press offices, had to respond.[2] There is, however, another type of crisis that not only directly involves government but results from plans or actions by the government, such as the U.S. invasion of Grenada in October 1983. The invasion came after my period of site observations; thus the following account of government/press relations in this crisis is based entirely on the public record. First, the chronology:[3]

Thursday, October 13	Prime Minister Maurice Bishop of Grenada put under house arrest by rival faction.
Wednesday, October 19	Bishop executed.
Thursday, October 20	White House meetings begin; naval task force diverted to waters off Grenada as "precautionary" move to protect Americans on the island.
Friday, October 21	Organization of Eastern Caribbean States (OECS) meets with Prime Ministers Tom Adams of Barbados and Edward Seaga of Jamaica to formulate a proposal for military intervention. President Reagan and Secretary of State Shultz leave for weekend in Augusta, Georgia.

Saturday, October 22	Shultz awakened (2:45 a.m.) with "informal request" from OECS for U.S. assistance. National Security Council (NSC) meets (9 a.m.); no firm decision taken.
Sunday, October 23	Reagan awakened (2:27 a.m.) and informed that U.S. Marine quarters in Beirut have been bombed with substantial loss of lives. NSC meets (9 a.m.), mostly about the Lebanon situation, but this also provides a cover to discuss Grenada. Late evening: Reagan signs order putting Grenada invasion plan into action.
Monday, October 24	CBS correspondent asks White House spokesman Speakes if a Grenada invasion is imminent; Speakes checks with NSC, replies to CBS, "preposterous." Monday night: congressional leaders and top press officers informed.[4]
Tuesday, October 25	Reagan enters White House briefing room (9:07 a.m.) and announces, "Early this morning, forces from six Caribbean democracies and the United States began a landing or landings on the island of Grenada." Eight hours after invasion Defense Secretary Weinberger holds Pentagon press conference, tells reporters they are not allowed to go to Grenada.
Wednesday, October 26	No reporters allowed on Grenada. White House briefings described as "acrimonious."
Thursday, October 27	U.S. military takes press pool of fifteen reporters to Grenada for the day.
Friday, October 28	Twenty-four reporters are taken to Grenada.
Saturday, October 29	Fifty reporters are taken to Grenada.
Tuesday, November 1	Defense Department says it has begun regular shuttle service for the press, leaving Barbados every four hours beginning at 8 a.m., returning from Grenada as soon as the plane can reload.
Thursday, November 3	New York Times headline: GRENADA FIGHTING IS ENDED.

The administration's press policy, which resulted in keeping most reporters off Grenada for sixty hours, provoked a confrontation with the press over some very basic issues. The government started with valid and vital concerns: the need for surprise, necessary for success in what could have been a delicate military and diplomatic undertaking; the security of information that should not be made known to enemies; and the efficiency of operations. But the press also had vital concerns. As an outside observer of government and the source of most information that Americans receive, the press is even more important than usual during periods of public distrust or cataclysmic events. The confrontation finally resolved itself to the issue of access.[5]

One apparent problem at the White House was that the president's spokesman had lied to reporters. After Larry Speakes was asked about a Grenada invasion on Monday afternoon by CBS's Bill Plante, he went to Captain Robert Sims, a navy public affairs specialist on the staff of the NSC; Sims went to Admiral John Poindexter, the deputy national security adviser. "Preposterous, knock it down hard," Poindexter is reported to have told Sims, who told Speakes, who used the word "preposterous" in replying to CBS. This became the party line and was repeatedly given to inquiring reporters by Speakes's deputy for foreign affairs, Les Janka. (Janka resigned on Monday, October 31, writing the president that "personal credibility is a precious asset.")[6]

From the vantage point of the press office the lie resulted from a series of errors for which Speakes could apologize and quickly reestablish his relatively good rapport with the reporters. In fact, the incident came close to destroying the usefulness to the president of his press operation. "Lying," however, was not the real issue, only the catalyst; as I noted earlier, most Washington reporters understand that there are some cases in which the government can justify honest lying.[7] Rather, what affected Speakes and his operatives much more was the public acknowledgment that they were not in the loop. In effect, the world had been told that the president and his top aides simply did not trust them enough or feel enough need of their services to keep them informed. In rank ordering, the Reagan press office would be the last to know. Reporters will say that they knew this all along. Perhaps. But they also have a vested interest in the White House press office. With the growth of the press corps and tightened security after the last attempt on the president's life, reporters are increasingly outsiders. Therefore, it becomes more important than ever for them to believe that they are dealing with press secretaries who have access to the inner circle. This increases the reporters' worth to their organizations and enhances their self-esteem.

Once the myth of the press secretary as insider has been shattered, the odds are long against putting the pieces together again. It is possible: partly as a result of having been kept in the dark about the Bay of Pigs invasion in 1961, Kennedy press secretary Pierre Salinger was informed in advance of the Cuban missile crisis in 1962, although he was still not a policy counselor.[8] But more likely there will be a reconciliation between press and press office only if a president is reelected.

According to news accounts, "President Reagan and Secretary of Defense Caspar W. Weinberger turned over control of the invasion almost completely to military officers once the President had given the go-ahead."[9] This was not disputed by the military; a headline in the *New York Times* for October 31 read, ADMIRAL SAYS IT WAS HIS DECISION TO TETHER THE PRESS. From the perspective of the military, no commander would want to be burdened with a cadre of reporters while he was busy doing his duty.[10] The military can hardly be faulted for making a military decision. But whether to exclude the press should have been a political decision. Although an eloquent essay by *Time*'s editor-in-chief, Henry Grunwald, strangely concluded that "trying to censor reality" was a "crude attempt by bureaucrats,"[11] what had happened was that political executives had abdicated their responsibility.

Certainly the most obvious consequence of excluding the press from Grenada for sixty hours was that reporters fiercely attacked the decision. As sociologist Michael Schudson notes, "wars are as good for journalists as for generals."[12] John Chancellor and David Brinkley later explained to a House Judiciary subcommittee that there is a long history of conventions between government and press that have allowed invasions to be covered, including Normandy in 1944, without compromising the military operations.[13] Yet the press did not claim that the military decision to keep the reporters off the island was unpopular with the public. As James Reston wrote, the administration "managed to persuade a lot of people that they had to choose between the security of the troops and the freedom of the press, and they chose security."[14] Still, as Vermont Royster noted, "Mr. Weinberger was lucky. All went well. Had things gone otherwise . . . [there] would have been a real public explosion."[15]

Blocked from being on the island, reporters sought other sources of information:

> Cuban media said six U.S. helicopter gunships pounded Cuban positions this morning (*Washington Post*, October 27).

> Subsequent reports obtained by The Miami Herald from ham operators said . . . (*Washington Post*, October 27).

> Reporters [at the press room in Bridgetown, Barbados] nervously fidget about, some talking on the phone to their editors, others pumping information out of one another (*Washington Post*, October 29).

> The senator added that the administration's case that the island was being readied to export revolution and terror in the eastern Caribbean was "inferential and circumstantial" at this point (*Washington Post*, October 29).

The president's policy, in short, had redirected the press to get its news from Radio Havana, amateur radio operators, rumor mills, and political opponents of the administration.[16] The price paid by the nation for the administration's press policy, therefore, was less accurate news. The price paid by the administration was fewer favorable stories.

On Thursday, October 27, television networks showed the first film from the island. On CBS, Dan Rather introduced the film as having been "shot by the army and censored by the army"; over the film itself, CBS superimposed "Cleared by Defense Department Censors." After the film, Rather twice more noted that the government had produced and "censored the film." The exclusion of reporters planted nagging doubts. Did events really happen the way the government said? This may be the most lasting consequence of the administration's action. As a former navy chief of information said of the media, "they have more credibility than any military spokesman ever will."[17]

PRESUMABLY the difference between a crisis by accident and a crisis by design is the amount of time that participants have to get ready. Yet in the Grenada invasion the government's press offices had little more notice than the Department of Transportation had knowledge that a plane was going to crash into the Fourteenth Street bridge. My hunch, however, is that the absence of a time distinction between these two types of crises on the level of press relations is not an aberration. The more the government wishes to maintain surprise and secrecy—and not only in military operations—the fewer people will be given a seat at the planning table. Last seated, in most instances, will be the press officer.

Indeed, press officers may turn out to be more useful in crises caused by accidents exactly because they cannot be excluded from advance planning. One reason Gosden could act so promptly at DOT was her close working relationship with Secretary Lewis. At the Pentagon in October 1983 there was no press officer in Secretary Weinberger's inner circle who could pound the table and tell the Joint Chiefs that their proposed handling of the reporters was unwise; at the White House the exclusion of Speakes was historically only different in degree. Considering the incident, Robert J. McCloskey wrote, "It ought to be an iron law that government spokesmen be there, as it was once said, at the takeoff as well as the landing. Regrettably it isn't."[18]

CHAPTER 6

Briefings

THE FIRST press officer arrives at the State Department's press office at 6:30 a.m. During the next hour Sandra McCarty reads the *New York Times*, the *Washington Post*, and the Baltimore *Sun*. Rush Taylor, director of the news operations, arrives a half hour after McCarty. He reads the wire services' printouts, the *Christian Science Monitor*, and the *Wall Street Journal*.[1] They are putting together the number one list, those news items on which the spokesman may wish to get instructions from the secretary of state at the 8:30 senior staff meeting; then they start on the number two list, questions that are considered likely to be asked by reporters at the daily briefing.[2] McCarty takes a call from her contact at the U.S. Information Agency who reports on various cables and Voice of America broadcasts. She reads a summary of television news programs. Spokesman Dean Fischer or Deputy Spokesman Alan Romberg comes back from Secretary Haig's meeting with additions for the list. By 9:30 the questions have been farmed out to the bureaus for "guidance," the term used to describe the short written statements that make up the briefing book. *

Thus begins a series of activities that serve two highly useful purposes. First, the briefing process is a valuable means of negotiating foreign policy positions within the government, mostly among the bureaus of the State Department but also interdepartmentally among State, Defense, and the White House. Second, the briefing process produces a collection of statements that are cabled around the world each day by mid-afternoon as part of the official foreign policy of the United States. These purposes are considerably removed from the initial intention of answering the questions of the reporters regularly assigned to the diplomacy beat. At the White House and Defense Department, on the other hand, the spokesmen's briefings retain their original purpose: they are a response—even if often an evasive one—to the demands of the press. Most other agencies of government, such as the FDA and

*See "Documents," p. 135.

61

the Department of Transportation, do not conduct regularly scheduled briefings.

In the press office of the Bureau of Near Eastern and South Asian Affairs, the reading and clipping begin at 7:00 a.m. The press office gets the *New York Times*, the *Washington Post*, the Baltimore *Sun*, the *Christian Science Monitor*, and the *Wall Street Journal*. Each bureau makes its own selections, but each selects almost the same newspapers. Copies of the bureau's *Morning Press Clippings* are distributed to the assistant secretary, the five deputy assistant secretaries, and the executive director. The bureau's public affairs adviser, Chris Ross, arrives at 7:45. His morning, he says, will be spent "feeding Dean's machine." He may be responsible for three items a week on the number one list and as many as nine questions a day on the number two list. Ross and his three assistants will write the routine guidances; others will come from the country desk officers, such as the director for Iran or the director for Egypt. All guidances from the bureau must be cleared by at least a deputy assistant secretary. NEA is only one of the nineteen units that feed into this system, but the five bureaus representing geographic areas account for well over 90 percent of the guidances; the others cover such subjects as human rights, terrorism, and international organizations.

On May 17, 1982, a typical day, the department press office directs questions for guidance to seven bureaus. The queries are prompted by seven stories from the *New York Times*, five from the *Washington Post*, two each from the *Christian Science Monitor* and Reuters, and single entries from UPI and the *Wall Street Journal*. The television networks are most likely to show up on Monday lists, reflecting news from the Sunday interview programs or "60 Minutes."

To illustrate the way guidances are expected to be written, press officer Bea Russell of the African Affairs Bureau invented the following example:

LOWER REVOLTA/MILITARY COUP

Q. What can you tell us about a reported military coup in Lower Revolta?
A. According to a radio broadcast monitored in Lisbon, President-for-Life Fernando Bangi-Olangi NMTBOBO (Hum-Bo-Bo) was overthrown August 19 by his nephew, Pepe Bangi-Olangi NMTBOBO, chief of staff of the army. The fate of the former dictator is unknown.
BACKGROUND: Lower Revolta, a collection of miniscule islands off the West Coast of Africa, formerly part of the Portuguese empire, became independent in 1975.
FYI ONLY: Conditions in Lower Revolta, which were never any great shakes, deteriorated rapidly under the ruthless leadership of President-for-Life NMTBOBO. The U.S. broke relations with Lower Revolta in 1976 after the U.S. Consul,

Sydney Hapless, disappeared under suspicious circumstances. The official Lower Revoltan government explanation that Mr. Hapless fell into the Hullabalubu (Hulla-ba-lu-boo) River and was devoured by crocodiles was not regarded as convincing by the Department of State.

The artificiality of a question-and-answer format tempts those who draft guidances to write questions that they can most easily answer rather than questions that are most likely to be asked. Henry Trewhitt, of the Baltimore *Sun*, jokes that a spokesman opens his briefing book and finds that the second question reads, "Let me rephrase my question. . . ."

As a guidance becomes more complicated or controversial, it requires more clearances. Each clearance is a form of negotiation: first within a bureau, then among bureaus, and finally with other agencies, notably the Pentagon and the National Security Council staff. Seven clearances were the most I saw on a single guidance; usually they had four clearances in addition to the initials of the drafter. The only guidances with a single clearance are routine announcements, such as the time and place of an impending speech by the secretary of state. The Lower Revolta military coup would have been a three-clearance guidance: drafted by the African Affairs press office and cleared by the country desk officer, the African Affairs bureau, and because of the Portuguese connection, by the Bureau of European Affairs press office.

During the forty-five minutes before the noon briefing, which starts around 12:30, the public affairs officers from the bureaus bring their guidances to the deputy spokesman's office where they move along a sort of assembly line, counterclockwise across the briefer's desk, as the briefer questions and comments: *Am I supposed to say this with a big smile? . . . What's our real view? . . . I'm not going to use it, we haven't got the clearances I want. It should have been looked at at the White House. . . . Will we get a lot of questions on this? . . . Did Haig say that?* [A call for verification.] *That's a slimy answer.*

The briefer (Fischer or Romberg) hands each guidance to Taylor on his right, who checks to see that the clearances are in order and then hands the guidance to Anita Stockman, the deputy director of news operations, who puts a copy in the briefing book, writes the subject in an index, and then hands a copy to Jake Gillespie of the USIA. There are about twenty-five guidances in the briefing book. Stockman makes up eleven sets for distribution; another set is added to the duty officer's book.

The preparation for the two daily White House briefings is more catch-as-catch-can as the press office staff phone their contacts in the agencies for data on whatever topics the press secretary thinks will be raised by the reporters.

Pentagon briefings in 1981–82 were held on Tuesdays and Thursdays at 11:30. However, when Melvin Laird was secretary of defense under Nixon, he scheduled daily briefings at 10:30, well before those at State and the White House. According to Jerry W. Friedheim, a Pentagon spokesman at that time, "this assured that . . . on most days all the government's press officers at least began their deliberations working off 'the Pentagon's piece of paper.'"[3] Defense Secretary Caspar Weinberger's spokesmen, Henry Catto and Benjamin Welles, are prepped for a session with reporters for an hour before the briefing; they review a stack of large index cards with questions and answers, first with the substantive experts, then with their own staff. Following the briefing, each card is returned to the officer who prepared it. He retains the card if he thinks the question is likely to come up again or discards it if this is unlikely. Clearly the cards are strictly for the purpose of briefing the briefer. At the State Department, on the other hand, the briefer's guidances are filed because they have been prepared as a record of U.S. policy.

REPORTERS start drifting into the State Department newsroom in late morning. They skim the press clippings from the Arms Control and Disarmament Agency (the State Department does not make a clipping service available to them). They check the AP, UPI, Reuters, and Foreign Broadcast Information Service tickers that are in a separate room. The newsroom fills up with discarded copies of the *Times* and the *Post*. Officials and reporters prepare for the briefing by reading and listening to the same news media. This becomes obvious when the questioning starts: *Do you have any comment on a story in the* New *York* Times *quoting some anonymous Cuban officials saying. . . . Dean, does the Department have any reaction to the report in the* Post *this morning about Iraq . . . There is a story running on one of the wires. . . . Dean, in the CBS special on Saturday, Ambassador Kirkpatrick said. . . .* Over a five-week period, the reporters mentioned specific news outlets in forty-six questions. The *New York Times* was the leader with nine; the *Washington Post* was mentioned five times (*New York Times* reporters tend to ask questions about *Times* stories). All television and radio combined were cited seven times: four were references to interview programs; the other three were to special reports as distinct from regular news broadcasts.

THE State Department briefing room became famous during the Iranian hostage crisis. TV nightly news showed the podium with its seal of the Department of State, the authority of the speaker further enhanced by a blue backdrop on which the world is a mustard-color silhouette. The briefer looks down a center aisle to a large clock, a bank of lights, and two rear platforms on which seven cameras are mounted. An aisle separates four rows of crescent-shaped desks. The desks grow longer as they move away from the podium, so that the six seats in the front are expanded to nine or ten by the last row. Desk microphones are activated by a man who sits on a raised platform facing the reporters. It is a room filled with symbols of pronouncements on world affairs.

Unlike White House briefings, there are no assigned seats at the State Department or the Pentagon, although young reporters seem to assume that the seniors are entitled to the front rows. The right to ask the first question and to end all department briefings are the prerogatives of the senior U.S. wire service reporter: Jim Anderson (UPI) at the State Department; Helen Thomas (UPI) at the White House; and Fred Hoffman (AP) at the Pentagon. Briefings typically last for half an hour, although during the three months that I attended State Department sessions, Anderson occasionally dismissed the briefer after fifteen minutes. Checking back to April 1980 when Secretary of State Vance resigned, I found some sessions that went on for over an hour.

The State Department briefings can be heard in various places throughout the building, at the White House, at the U.S. Mission to the UN in New York, and at the foreign press centers in Washington and New York. There is an impression among some reporters that this makes a difference, elevating the discourse to a higher role in policymaking, notably because Secretary Kissinger was said to have been a devoted listener when he was at his desk. James Lobe of Inter Press Service, a wire service that stresses third world news, says he designed questions to reach this hidden audience. But officials deny that these internal broadcastings have any direct impact on policymaking. After I listened from several locations, I found the denials plausible, if only because so much is lost to the auditor who is not in the briefing room.[4]

The Carter administration's decision to permit a live television feed from the daily State Department briefings is usually called a watershed dividing the history of briefings into two epochs. The question of whether television makes any difference in the conduct and consequence of briefings has almost passed beyond recall. Diplomats and print journalists blame the cameras for luring the crowds that have turned the briefings into a circus, for making the briefers less frank because of their concern about being on TV or more simplistic because of their desire to be on TV, and for making the questioning more combative, longwinded, and bizarre. And even if all these things have not happened, say print journalists, they will—just wait until the number of cameras increases exponentially with the expansion of cable television. An irony, perhaps, is that the unprofessional behavior comes from print reporters; TV reporters usually know how to behave when the cameras are on.

Television's presence is too easy an explanation for what has happened to the briefings. In pre TV days the spokesmen repeated for the cameras in mid-afternoon the highlights of the sessions. Comparing then and now probably would show little difference in content as a result of one's being "rehearsed" and the other "spontaneous." Nor have spokesmen misspoken enough either to have created additional news or to have embarrassed the government. Moreover, the tendentiousness of the briefings, according to Bernard Gwertzman of the *New York Times*, began before the TV cameras were there, in 1965 when President Johnson sent marines into the Dominican Republic, and it escalated along with the war in Vietnam. Even the increased attendance at the briefings, recalls former Deputy Spokesman Thomas Reston, began not when the cameras were initially turned on but when the Iranians took over the U.S. embassy. At the White House, where the briefings are not televised, the proceedings are far more raucous.

Indeed, it is the decorum of the State Department briefings that is so notable—and often in stark contrast to the content. No matter how outrageous the questioning by marginal journalists, the regulars listen politely. Marvin Kalb of NBC commented, "In all the years I've been here I don't think I've lost my temper three times. What good would it do?" The reporters do not shout. They apologize if they inadvertently cut off a colleague. The quiet laughter is as if a joke's punchline had been in Latin. Diplomatic correspondents see themselves engaged in delicate negotiations over what the department is willing to put on the record.

Q. Could you say what the U.S. position is on the applicability of the Rio Treaty to the Falklands dispute?
A. It would be speculative and hypothetical to get into that area. . . .
Q. Not premature?
A. That too, John.

Pentagon briefings, scheduled for twice a week but dropped on days that the secretary of defense is testifying before Congress or is out of town, are less like negotiations and more like combat.

Q. And you sent the air force back to the drawing board because . . .
A. Not to the drawing board, just to evaluate those proposals. It's an evaluation. It's not a drawing board. Everything is designed.

Q. Okay, I stand corrected on my terminology. You sent the air force back to restudy . . .

A. No, to reevaluate. Be explicit. You're a newspaperman.

White House briefings resemble a fraternity party. Reporters mostly shout, laugh, and interrupt.

Q. [Will the president] definitely sign it by July?

A. Okay. Wait a minute. Now back up. Listen very carefully.

Q. Let Larry finish his answer.

A. That's really getting out of hand. I noticed in the briefing yesterday, I never got to finish an answer, and I probably had something that would be earth-shattering there on the tail end.

Q. Let us know from now on.

Q. What was your answer?

A. I don't know. I forgot. . . . Okay, you've got the fat bill with a billion dollars that is coming down here today, which I would anticipate the president will veto. Then you have the so-called skinny bill which is also the short bill.

Q. Short and skinny?

A. Yes, short and skinny bill. It . . .

Q. Is that . . .

A. Now, see, I didn't get through it. I didn't get through it. I didn't get through it. Do you really want to know or you'd rather not?

Differences among the briefings may simply reflect the personality of each beat, with reporters taking on the characteristics of those they cover, as columnist Russell Baker once contended.[5] The State Department, thinks Leslie Gelb, "is the strongest socializing agent in town." If, indeed, there is a self-selection process at work in determining which reporter ultimately gets which assignment, then presumably the diplomatic choose to cover the State Department, the combative are intrigued by the military, and the political want to be around the White House. As the same rough rule of thumb, there could be similar forces at work in the selection of briefers. Certainly a president is handicapped without a politically engaging press secretary, and a secretary of state is benefited by a spokesman who is capable of obfuscation in the most elegant language. When watching the minuet danced by briefers and reporters, I thought I observed that when the regular diplomatic reporters least approved the State Department's policy and conduct, they were most formal and polite in the manner in which they framed their questions— quite the opposite of how military reporters responded when they were out of sorts with the Pentagon.

Robert Pierpoint, who has been a regular at the White House and State Department, also argues that behavior depends on the degree to which information is available to reporters. When presidential aides begin to hunker down, Pierpoint says, "the White House briefing may be the only shot we'll get at a story," and the level of aggressiveness rises. The reporters are responding to officials' actions that they see as a threat to the way they can do their jobs. Similarly, reporters who are least likely to be invited in for interviews at the State Department will try to make more assertive use of the briefings.

THE State Department briefing room is always filled to capacity, about seventy reporters, and seems to divide into thirds: mainstream U.S. press; foreign correspondents; and others, mostly from fringe operations, some of whom come every day, some of whom show up to check a rumor that may affect the price of gold, as in the case of a biweekly commodities newsletter. Each group has its own agenda.

The U.S. reporters on daily deadline, notably those from the wire services and the TV networks, expect little more than an on-the-record quotation to fit in their stories as the department's official position on the world's top crisis. Less privileged reporters hope that the questioning will help direct them to what they should be covering. Those reporters who have private ways to get answers but are expected by their employers to attend the briefings pass the time practicing "nuance journalism." This is different from "trap the briefer," in which the regulars at the White House try to get the press secretary to reveal information that they think he wants to keep secret. Nuance questioning requires being able to compare day-to-day changes in the department's guidances. The reporters then seek implications, which they uncover through Talmudic analysis of text:

> Q. Do you have any comment on the current situation on the West Bank?
> A. [Reading the guidance:] We are increasingly concerned over the heightened level of tensions, demonstrations, and especially use of lethal force. . . .
> Q. Dean . . . yesterday you didn't . . . use the adverb "especially," did you?
> A. It'll be a simple matter for you to compare them.
> Q. But we don't wish to signal by the use of that adverb that we are taking particular notice. . . .

The questioner is right in this case. He has spotted a seven-clearance guidance, personally approved by the assistant secretary of the Bureau of Near Eastern and South Asian Affairs; had the adverb been considered less important, an okay by the deputy assistant secretary might well have been sufficient.

When this game is properly played by reporters and officials, a U.S. position can be accurately beamed to interested parties without the government's having to take elaborate diplomatic action, as when John M. Goshko of the *Washington Post* reported this cue on April 22, 1982: "The United States, striving to avoid recriminations that could affect Israel's scheduled withdrawal Sunday from the Sinai Peninsula, reacted to yesterday's bombing of Lebanon with a low-key statement . . . so bland that it seemed almost identical to expressions of concern routinely issued by the department. . . ."

Yet as I became more familiar with the process from inside government, watching the hurried production of daily guidances, I could see reporters finding nuances that had not been meant to be nuances (*Q. How do you use the word "negotiations" versus "talks"? A. I tend to use the terms interchangeably*). Reporters credited more facility in the subtleties of language to the collectivity that is the State Department than it is entitled to. At other times press officers had to seek out selected reporters to let them know that something said had been meant to be a nuance. Veteran reporters argue that the briefer, not the system, is at fault. I watched two briefers and read the transcripts of two others, all said to be variously skilled, and what impressed me, despite the obvious differences, primarily in the use of humor and the degree to which they chose to be advocates, was the relative sameness of the level of information. The briefers could set somewhat different tones, but because they were not free agents, their basic messages were etched by the bureaus.

Nuance journalism is not a game played by foreign correspondents. The Western Europeans might have been the exception had not the noon hour conflicted with their deadlines. A few others are proficient enough in English and have been in the country long enough, but in the main the foreign reporters in Washington receive nuances secondhand from reading the elite U.S. press. I saw Russian reporters at the State Department briefings only when the subject was going to be the Soviet's use of chemical warfare in Southeast Asia. The large Japanese contingent only came in force when their foreign minister was in Washington. Generally, then, these were journalists who were there when their countries were on the world's front burners that day and who were hardly disinterested observers:[6]

Q. [Joseph Polakoff, formerly of the Jewish Telegraphic Agency] Would you call these people who throw rocks, who throw hand grenades and in other ways inflict injury upon those soldiers or those people who are trying to maintain peace, would you call them demonstrators as if they were children marching in a parade with placards?
A. I'm not trying to call them anything. I gave you the statement I have on the West Bank, and I'm just not going to go beyond it.
Q. How would you refer to these people who throw hand grenades and rocks?

A. Joe, I'm just not going to go beyond what I gave you.

Q. Would you say that it's a fair term to call them demonstrators?

A. There is nothing more I intend to say, Joe.

Q. [Abdul Salam Massaruen, Arab-American Media Service] At this point, Dean, since these people who are on occupied territories are occupied, anybody around the world could deprive the occupied people from resisting the occupation if it resorts to military power, killing, murdering, and destroying the property and the lives of human beings. Is there a way that you could say that the Palestinian people who are in the [inaudible] have no right to resist even if they were to resort to force?

A. Again, I must repeat that I gave you the statement that I wish to on the West Bank, and I'm going to stick with it.

Israeli and Egyptian reporters are embarrassed by this type of exchange. "We do not ask unprofessional questions," says Shalom Kital of the Israel Broadcasting Authority. A similar disclaimer was made by Adib Andrawis of the Middle East News Agency, the Cairo-based wire service. Still, increasingly the rancor from some troubled part of the world spills over into the noon briefing, and rarely does this questioning have anything to do with a reply from the spokesman. Mainstream U.S. correspondents, who are annoyed by this waste of their time, make no attempt to shut off the "debate," although they may ask for a filing break, which permits them to leave the room.

The final third of those attending are representatives of minute specialized publications, free lancers, world conspiracy theorists, a defrocked Foreign Service officer, agent provocateurs for the PLO and similar movements, visitors to Washington, and political ideologues of the right and left.[7]

Q. [Stanley Ezrol, *Executive Intelligence Review*, a magazine founded by Lyndon H. LaRoche, Jr.] As long as we're on the subject of coups, there are reports in *Europeo* that a large number of British intelligence operatives have entered Sicily, and are working in collaboration with the Sicilian Mafia to foment destabilization and disruptions in the area. The report goes on to say that on the United States end, this is being coordinated by the inheritors of the old relationship between the United States intelligence operations and the Sicilian Mafia. Those inheritors who are named are David Rockefeller, Henry Kissinger, and Alexander Haig. Do you have any comment on that?

A. Well, the secretary is obviously in good company. [Laughter] Of course I have no comment on that. It's an outrageous allegation.

Q. Let me ask one more. The secretary is very open and speaks very fondly about his association with the Trilateral Commission membership, both in Europe and the United States. You here have been rather testy about the secretary's relationship with the Propaganda Two Lodge in Italy. Now, given the overlapping membership between the Propaganda Two Lodge and the Trilateral Commission in Italy, and given the almost total identity of political policies and purposes between the two, why is it that the secretary is so open on that question, and you have been so defensive?

A. I try to avoid being testy, but sometimes temptation just overwhelms me.

During a debriefing in late May 1982, Rush Taylor commented to the press office staff, "that was every nut that we have [in there] today, including [a woman who was] stretched out on the floor."

A sensible briefing may cover up to seven subjects and focus on not more than two; when the nuts are there in full force, the number of subjects can jump to twenty. Aside from the day's automatic story, the clearest predictor of what subjects will be raised is which marginal reporters show up: the presence of a particular gadfly, for instance, almost ensures a question about slavery in Mauritania. Some serious reporters would like the State Department to limit attendance; most, however, recognize the problems inherent in having government determine who should be recognized as a journalist. The department's position is that the press corps should police itself as it once did. But when the State Department Correspondents Association was threatened with lawsuits, it withdrew from the credentialing business. Press passes now merely require a letter from an American news organization stating that the reporter is an employee; foreign correspondents need a letter from the embassy of the country in which their organization is based.

After the senior wire service reporter ends the formal briefing, reporters gather around the podium for a postbriefing briefing, a few minutes of on-background questions and answers. The fiction behind the practice is that the spokesman will be more frank now that the cameras have been turned off. Nodding at the group surrounding the briefer, a mainstream reporter asks, "Do you think they all know what 'background' means?" He considers the answer both self-evident and an explanation of what has happened to State Department briefings.

Size, not television, explains most of what has caused the decline in the briefings as a tool of serious journalism. In terms of intelligence and competence, TV network correspondents at key locations in Washington are the equals of reporters for the prestigious newspapers and magazines. There is no distinction between electronic and print journalists in the quality of questions. Rather, the decline in quality has come from the fringes, from reporters for marginal and sometimes questionable operations, who, along with the growth in their numbers, have also become more vocal.

THE PUBLIC affairs officer at the Bureau of Near Eastern and South Asian Affairs sits in his office listening to the briefing, which he then summarizes for distribution within the bureau: "*West Bank Demonstrations*: Fischer reads guidance. Asked isn't it the same as yesterday. Asked if word 'especially' was added. Fischer referred to statement he read." At the Bureau of Inter-

American Affairs, Public Affairs Adviser Jeff Biggs also listens to briefings. He hears Alan Romberg announce that a charter airline "has been designated as a Cuban national for purposes of the Trading with the Enemy Act" (April 19, 1982). Biggs then calls the Treasury Department to make sure that the release has been put out. He takes a call from a *Miami Herald* reporter: no, he explains, this is not a ban on flying to Cuba; other companies fly there.

In the deputy spokesman's office, where the guidances had been assembled, the press officers convene for a short debriefing, not more than ten minutes: NEA *wants us to reiterate our definition of cease-fire . . . that was a good question . . . the land reform guidance was somewhat misleading, we'll write a clarification . . . he always asks strange questions.* The primary purpose of the session is to make sure that all the questions on which the briefer has promised written answers—so-called taken questions—have been noted for action by the appropriate bureaus.* Today the briefer has agreed to provide answers to six inquiries; eight was the record during the period I observed.

The USIA representative has been annotating his copies of the guidances during the briefing. He reports to his agency's policy people at a 2:30 meeting. The government's daily line then will be cabled to all U.S. embassies throughout the world.

The officials and reporters now go to lunch, usually at the department's cafeteria. Reporters from the TV networks sit together, and others who join them are from elite publications or have exceptionally long tenure on the beat. Foreign correspondents sit together, and arrange themselves by language and region. Reporters from marginal operations sit together and divide by ideology. The food is not very good, but reporters say it is a good place to cadge information from officials. The reporters and officials sit at separate tables and rarely mix.

BRIEFINGS play a minor role in the Pentagon routine during peacetime. There are relatively few reporters in the building compared to the number of generals and admirals, and experienced journalists need not be forced to rely on an organized approach to getting information. But at the White House the mechanism of the briefing—including special briefings by outside experts—is growing as a way of containing the burgeoning press corps. At this level of government, according to Congressman Richard Cheney who was President Ford's chief of staff, "reporters sop up executives' time."

The White House press office added a second daily briefing in 1981,

*See "Documents," p. 134.

initially as a response to the TV networks' need for faster information following the March 30 attempt on the president's life. Reporters who show up at 9:15 a.m. in the press secretary's office are primarily from organizations that can afford to assign more than one person to the beat. In May 1982 there were usually about twenty reporters at the morning briefing and between fifty and sixty at the noon briefing. Serendipitously, the White House thus created a smaller, more informal briefing that mainstream reporters like because it is not yet consumed by the idiosyncratic behavior of reporters from the outskirts of journalism. White House press officers also like the early session because they feel it gives them a better crack at steering reporters in the direction of their top story. But State Department officials are troubled: "These early-morning briefings cause us more substantive problems than all other institutionalized exchange between government and the press. . . . The White House briefers frequently give spontaneous or simplistic answers to complex foreign policy issues without having their responses cleared in advance by the policymakers."

This remark reflects what the State Department now sees as the purpose of the briefings: a clearance mechanism for official reactions to world events. The briefings have been coopted by government officials and are only secondarily related to the reporters' needs. The frustration of the mainstream reporter over this development is expressed by the UPI's Jim Anderson: "The 'noon news briefing,' like the 'German Democratic Republic,' is now a complete misnomer: It does not take place at noon; it rarely produces news; and, in view of the lack of information, it is not brief."[8] Routine announcements are made—*an assistant secretary will testify tomorrow before a House committee . . . a speech text will be available in the press office at 3:00 p.m.* A snippet of a spokesman's comment can add texture to a radio or television story.

The main utility of the noon briefing is that it forces the U.S. foreign ministry to turn out a written statement on every diplomatic issue that is apt to be in the front section of the morning's *New York Times*. The guidances may be murky or merely "no comment." A USIA executive regrets that they are not elaborate arguments for U.S. policy. But producing them at all is no small accomplishment—no other unit of government does anything approaching this. A wide range of positions is negotiated, sometimes with other agencies, before noon. By midafternoon they have been cabled to all posts abroad, forming a web of connective tissue between headquarters and those in the field who are expected to know where their government stands on subjects beyond their purview.

State Department briefings may once have been intended as a useful service for the regulars on the beat. They may once have been a response to reporters' needs. They no longer are. Unlike the Pentagon, the State Department now produces guidances even on days when there are no briefings and no reporters have gathered. The message is not the media; the media provide the excuse for producing the message.

CHAPTER 7

Leaks and Other Informal Communications

Langhorne A. Motley, the new Assistant Secretary of State for Inter-American Affairs, told a Congressional committee last week that departmental efforts to consult with the lawmakers on Central American policy had been disrupted by "premature unauthorized partial disclosure" of plans.

"Do you mean leaks?" one member of the panel asked.

"Yes," Mr. Motley replied.[1]

AFTER information comes through the formal channels—press release, speech text, public document, news conference, briefing, interview, and observation of an event—reporters gather additional information through informal means that have come to be lumped together as leaks.

The leak deserves a better fate than to share a common definition with rumor, gossip, and other back-channel exchanges between sources and reporters. As defined by Motley, a leak is a "premature unauthorized partial disclosure," as distinguished from a "premature authorized partial disclosure," which is a plant. Or, depending on one's vantage point, a plant is a beneficial leak.

The leak is rarely a tool of press offices, whose domain is the formal channels of information. Robert Pierpoint of CBS says that during the six presidencies he covered, a White House press secretary only once leaked information to him. The primary reason spokesmen try to stay out of the leaking business, according to former presidential press secretary George Reedy, is that "since manipulation of the press involves favoritism to some newsmen it inevitably creates antagonism among others."[2]

Nor is leaking often practiced in the lower civil service. The bureaucrats' world faces inward. They know best how to maneuver within their own agencies; journalists, except possibly for some specialized reporters, are outside their ken and represent risk beyond possible gain.

75

The U.S. Constitution, however, provides reporters with a legislative branch in which they can always find someone who will enjoy sharing the president's secrets with them. John Goshko, who reports from the State Department for the *Washington Post*, recalls that a good story came from a congressional staff member who was talking to a *Post* congressional reporter, Margot Hornblower, who then told Goshko. "When the congressional staffer read the story he could never have known that he was the source," says Goshko. According to a wise departmental press officer, "we just assume that anything given to the Hill will be leaked and act accordingly." It is a painful lesson for presidents to learn. Reagan briefs his leaders in the House and Senate on what will be in his State of the Union message and the next day reads David Broder's story on the front page of the *Post*: "Neither [Howard] Baker nor [Robert] Michel would elaborate on the contents, preserving the secrecy the White House hopes to maintain until Reagan gives his address to Congress and the nation next Tuesday. But sources on Capitol Hill said it would probably include. . . ."[3]

Perhaps the greatest frustration for presidents is when they are forced to realize that most executive branch leakers are their own people—political appointees—rather than the faceless bureaucrats they campaigned against.[4] "A government," as James Reston was first to note, "is the only known vessel that leaks from the top."[5] This chapter, then, steps outside the book's framework to describe the part of the government/press connection that takes place outside of the press offices.

From the journalists' point of view, writes Tom Wicker, "What Presidents are apt to consider leaks . . . are often more nearly the result of good work by reporters diligent and intelligent enough to ask the right questions of the right sources at the right time."[6] Former Secretary of State Dean Rusk offers a hypothetical example of how the process can work:

> A reporter is leaving the State Department at the end of the day when he sees the Soviet ambassador's car drive up. Figuring that the ambassador has brought a message, the reporter gives the machinery a chance to work, then starts calling around. After being told he's on the wrong track at several offices, he gets to the fellow on Berlin, who has been told never to lie directly to the press. The reporter says, "John, I understand that the Soviet ambassador has just come in with a message on Berlin." So the man says, "Sorry, I can't say a thing about it. Can't help you on that." Ah! He's got it. In the absence of an absolute denial, he's on the track. He figures out what the Berlin problem looks like and then calls a friend at the Soviet embassy. "By the way," he says, "what's the attitude of the Soviet Union on this particular point on Berlin?"

He listens for a few moments, then he [writes] his story [for] the next morning
on the message the Soviet ambassador brought in about Berlin.

The chances are that the president will call the secretary of state and ask,
"Who in the hell has been leaking news over at the Department of State?"[7]

It is a "curious delusion among upper bureaucrats and high officials," Stewart
Alsop concluded in 1968, "that a reporter cannot possibly reach the same
rather obvious conclusions that government officials reached unless the
reporter has had illicit access to secret information."[8]

Viewed from inside government, a typology of why leakers leak would
include:

The Ego Leak: giving information primarily to satisfy a sense of self-
importance; in effect, "I am important because I can give you information
that is important." This type of leak is popular with staff, who have fewer
outlets for ego tripping. Assistants like to tell (and embellish) tales of struggle
among their superiors. I believe ego is the most frequent cause of leaking,
although it may not account for the major leaks. Other Washington observers disagree. Many reporters and officials prefer to think of leaks as more
manipulative and mysterious, but this, of course, also serves their egos.

The Goodwill Leak: a play for a future favor. The primary purpose is to
accumulate credit with a reporter, which the leaker hopes can be spent at a
later date. This type of leak is often on a subject with which the leaker has
little or no personal involvement and happens because most players in
governmental Washington gather a great deal of extraneous information in
the course of their business and social lives.

The Policy Leak: a straightforward pitch for or against a proposal using
some document or insiders' information as the lure to get more attention
than might be otherwise justified. The great leaks, such as the Pentagon
papers in 1971, often fit in this category.

The Animus Leak: used to settle grudges. Information is disclosed to
embarrass another person.

The Trial-Balloon Leak: revealing a proposal that is under consideration
in order to assess its assets and liabilities. Usually proponents have too much
invested in a proposal to want to leave it to the vagaries of the press and
public opinion. More likely, those who send up a trial balloon want to see
it shot down, and because it is easier to generate opposition to almost anything
than it is to build support, this is the most likely effect.

The Whistle-Blower Leak: unlike the others, usually employed by career
personnel. Going to the press may be the last resort of frustrated civil servants

who feel they cannot correct a perceived wrong through regular government channels. Whistle blowing is not synonymous with leaking; some whistle blowers are willing to state their case in public.[9]

LEAKS can be meant to serve more than one purpose, which complicates attempts to explain the motivation behind a particular leak. An ego leak and a goodwill leak need not be mutually exclusive; a policy leak also could work as an animus leak, especially since people on each side of a grudge tend to divide along policy lines; and all leaks can have policy implications regardless of motive.

Beyond the basic leaks, experienced reporters and officials enjoy trying to identify elaborate variations, such as "the daring reverse leak, an unauthorized release of information apparently for one reason but actually accomplishing the opposite," says Hugh Heclo.[10] A candidate for this distinction was Bob Woodward's *Washington Post* story on February 19, 1982, that reported on notes taken by a participant in Alexander Haig's senior staff meetings. Among the revelations were that the U.S. secretary of state called the British foreign secretary, Lord Carrington, a "duplicitous bastard," and that in private Haig had a much grimmer assessment of U.S. prospects in the Middle East than he had in public. Most initial reaction was that the notes had come from someone who was out to get Haig. But on February 22, William Safire presented an alternative suggestion in his *New York Times* column: Woodward was investigating a disturbing question—"Was it true that Al had gone bonkers?"—and the leaker was a Haig loyalist who felt a plausible selection of notes could show that his boss was of sound mind and in command. Former State Department Spokesman Robert McCloskey, who had become the *Post*'s ombudsman, wrote that the leak was "dishonorable" and that the leaker was a "villain." If Woodward knew "whether the source's motive was benign or mischievous . . . [he] had an obligation to share it with the reader."[11] The reporters I interviewed, on the other hand, argue that the leaker's motivation need not concern them, only whether a story is true.

A year later, Safire's theory had become the conventional wisdom in Washington.[12] Correct or not, it undoubtedly will be a permanent and cherished addition to the insiders' mythology of leaks. But few reporters, officials, or scholars ever mention "the no-purpose leak," based solely on the gregarious nature of politicians. In the opinion of a *New York Times* reporter, "on the Hill they talk because they love to talk."

THE WINTER of Ronald Reagan's discontent with the press began in late October of his first year in office, perhaps a bit delayed in historical terms because of the March 30 assassination attempt. This section traces the turmoil of November and December 1981 and January 1982. Understanding all the major battles that were fought through the press during this period gives one a better sense of the uses of leaks and other informal means of communication than if special cases had been chosen. The period coincides with the fine tuning of the president's annual budget proposals in a mid-term election year, always a busy time for intrigue. Although not typical in intensity, these months do reflect the standard array of conflicts that are reported from Washington, beginning with high-level personality clashes.

> Among the rumors of change, one features a grand game of musical chairs: Meese for Defense in place of Weinberger, who then takes Haig's place at State, with Haig's deputy—William Clark, a former Reagan aide in California—moving to the White House in place of Meese and Allen. . . .
>
> Joseph Kraft, *Washington Post*,
> October 27, 1981

> Although White House spokesmen won't confirm it, one scenario being discussed in the back channels has top White House aide Ed Meese eventually being shifted to the Pentagon to replace Defense Secretary Weinberger, who would shift to State to replace Secretary Haig. White House National Security Adviser Allen would be assigned duty elsewhere. His post would either be reduced in rank or, perhaps, filled by a career foreign service officer, such as Philip Habib.
>
> Bob Schieffer, "CBS Evening News,"
> October 28, 1981

The president was obviously annoyed. As reporters walked with him across the White House south lawn to a waiting helicopter on October 29, he said that Kraft and Schieffer were "blowing smoke [and] also doing a disservice to this country. I am very happy with the team we have . . . we're all getting along fine, and there's going to be no musical chairs being played."

Rumors of such a high order, popping up simultaneously in two major news outlets, "are almost always intended to damage the political fortunes or alter the policy views of the chosen victim," *New York Times* reporter Leslie Gelb noted several days later, "and they are almost always untrue—at least when first disseminated."[13] The beauty of the musical-chairs rumor was that it was aimed at both the national security adviser and the secretary of state. Thus it reflected the hostility of almost everyone in Washington. Those who were against either Haig or Allen included most of the White House, State Department, Pentagon, and Congress. Yet the rumor was too grand to be anything but the talk of White House corridors. That it eventually turned out to be semiaccurate—Haig and Allen were removed from public life within a year—needed a great deal of assistance from the two men. Allen obliged his critics by having been shown to have accepted $1,000 and several watches from a Japanese magazine as a thank-you for arranging an interview with Mrs. Reagan. The revelations led to his departure from government, but that departure was not related to institutional, personality, or policy disputes with the secretary of state. Haig's problems within the administration were of a different order.

On Saturday afternoon, October 31, David Gergen at the White House obtained an advance copy of a syndicated column that was scheduled to appear on Tuesday, November 3, in which Jack Anderson put Haig's name on the top of the president's "disappointment list." According to unnamed White House sources, "the secretary of state reportedly has one foot on a banana and could skid right out of the Cabinet before summer." As the administration's director of communications, Gergen phoned Anderson to request a disclaimer in that the president had repeatedly said he retained confidence in his secretary of state. Gergen then told Haig about the impending column.

Haig called Anderson twice during the day. He was "angry and upset," said the columnist, and indicated that the attack on him "was obviously the handiwork of a top White House aide, who had been running a guerrilla campaign against him for nine months." Anderson then rewrote his column to include this new information. Anderson's wide readership and the type of exposé that he specializes in give him some influence. But unlike the chief diplomatic correspondent of the New York Times, secretaries of state need not notice Anderson in order to perform their stately duties nor do embassies cable the muckraker's views to their foreign ministries. However, the State Department, through its spokesman, confirmed that Haig was accurately quoted, which ensured that the Anderson column would be noticed by media powers and the foreign ministries that are important to a secretary of state.

On November 4, a front-page headline in the New York Times announced, HAIG CHARGES A REAGAN AIDE IS UNDERMINING HIM. Between the headline and Bernard Gwertzman's story, there was also a three-column photograph of Reagan, Haig, and Allen. The Washington Post had the story on page 1 for two days (Anderson's column was on page B15). The Post articles by Don Oberdorfer and Martin Schram rehearsed in detail the conflict between Haig and the White House staff since the president's inauguration, including, most recently, how Haig had confronted White House Chief of Staff Baker about the Schieffer and Kraft stories. The reporters concluded, "the disputes, at times occurring publicly, seemed to be personal infighting rather than struggles over ideology."[14]

The "Guerrilla Campaign Controversy," as it was called by the *Post*, was still on the front page when Haig became embroiled in another dispute. Testifying before the Senate Foreign Relations Committee, he said, "there are contingency plans in the NATO doctrine to fire a nuclear weapon for demonstrative purposes." The statement was an aside, meant to illustrate a point. The next day, November 5, the secretary of defense, testifying before the Senate Armed Services Committee, replied, "there is absolutely nothing in any of the plans with which I am familiar that contains anything remotely resembling this, nor should be." Responding to Senator John W. Warner, Republican of Virginia, Weinberger was clearly expecting the question. By late afternoon, David Gergen resolved the matter: "Both were correct fundamentally."[15] Nevertheless, film clips of Haig and Weinberger, separated by a twenty-six-word bridge on the "NBC Nightly News," created a compelling drama.

The president summoned Haig and Allen to the Oval Office on November 5, just as he would shortly have to summon David Stockman: "going to the woodshed," Stockman called the experience. In both cases, Reagan emerged to blame the press. "Sometimes I wonder if there is such a thing as an unnamed source," said the president, using his more-in-sorrow voice. Columnist Safire replied, "The truth, as any Washington reporter will attest, is that it is hard to avoid being buttonholed by high White House aides complaining about the turfbuilding Mr. Haig, or by State officials running down Richard Allen and (more gingerly) Defense Secretary Weinberger. . . . These sources are neither 'sinister forces' nor 'unnamed'—they may be unidentified, but they have real names—and are not figments of journalistic imaginations, as Mr. Reagan suggested."[16] The *Chicago Tribune*, noting that the "public whining of some of the president's top foreign policy officials is becoming a disgrace," lectured the foreign policy establishment to "stop this infantile wrangling."[17]

Less than a week later, on November 11, new shock waves hit the administration when advance copies of the December issue of *The Atlantic* arrived in Washington. Its lead article was "The Education of David Stockman" by William Greider. Stockman, a former Republican congressman from Michigan, had been appointed to his cabinet-level job as the director of the Office of Management and Budget after pledging public fealty to supply-side economics; Greider was an assistant managing editor of the

Washington Post. For over eight months the conservative official and the liberal journalist had been meeting, and there were eighteen tape-recorded interviews to prove it. The length of the article, nearly 18,000 words, guaranteed that most people would learn its contents from news reports. Reporters, naturally, highlighted the most unexpected Stockman quotations. "None of us really understand what's going on with all these numbers," he said about the president's budget. Later he said that the Kemp-Roth bill, the president's tax proposal "was always a Trojan horse to bring down the top rate," suggesting that its purpose was to lower the taxes that the rich must pay. "The rest of it is a secondary matter." On the bargaining that produced the tax legislation: "Do you realize the greed that came to the forefront? The hogs were really feeding." Could Stockman have been misquoted or sand-bagged by a wily adversary? The November 12 headline in the *New York Daily News* read, STOCKMAN IS MUGGED BY MAG. No, said Stockman, Greider had not acted in bad faith. "In early September, at our last meeting," Greider later wrote, "I again reminded him that I was preparing to publish the full account of our conversation, and again he assented."[18]

Greider said that as an editor he was getting "a valuable peephole on the inner policy debates of the new administration," but what did Stockman expect to gain? Greider said he assumed Stockman felt he was getting "a valuable connection with an important newspaper . . . [that he could use] to prod and influence the focus of our coverage."[19] If so, it turned out to be a bad deal for the president, who, after all, had not been a party to the bargain.

Once again the wounds of an administration were self-inflicted. Presidents have a right to try to conduct their internal business in an orderly manner and to try to time their moves to their advantage. This need not be of high concern to reporters, but the cabinet and the White House staff are a president's employees, presumably expected to be loyal and discreet. When leaving the administration in December 1981, Reagan's political adviser, Lyn Nofziger, said, "It seems to me that some people in talking to the media forget that when they are putting out information that may be hurtful to another member of the Administration, that what they are doing is hurting the President."[20]

FORCE IN CENTRAL AMERICA OPPOSED

by James McCartney [Knight-Ridder newspapers]
Philadelphia Inquirer, December 3

Haunted by memories of Vietnam, the Defense Department is strongly opposing White House and State Department threats to use military force to halt what the administration perceives as subversion by leftist forces in Central America.

McCartney, a veteran on the national security affairs beat, was surprised that this was the lead story in the Defense Department's early bird news clips. It was not new news, he readily admitted. Leslie Gelb had had a front page story in the *New York Times* a month earlier in which Haig was said to have "been pressing the Pentagon to examine a series of options for possible military action in El Salvador and against Cuba and Nicaragua," while the military was said to be opposing military action. Also on November 5, just after the president had told Haig and Allen to stop squabbling, Hedrick Smith of the *Times* had an interview with the secretary of state in which he "indirectly confirmed" Gelb's story.

Given all the talk of military options, McCartney had gone to the Pentagon to ask very specific questions about matters like "interdicting supplies." Instead he was directed to "a certain guy who volunteered to flesh out my questions into 'a broader perspective.'" McCartney later said, "He was answering questions I hadn't asked." The Defense Department wished to advertise a policy disagreement with the State Department. This was not a personal feud. McCartney noted, "They hadn't tried to sell me a story in the first place." He walked through the door and they saw an opportunity to make a pitch for their position. His article led off the Pentagon news clips on December 3 partly because copies of the *New York Times* happened to arrive late; being in the early bird edition, however, attracted the attention of other reporters, who told me they planned to write stories about the dispute.

U.S. SEARCH IS ON FOR 5 TERRORISTS
REPORTED PLANNING TO KILL REAGAN

by Philip Taubman
New York Times, December 4

The Government has received detailed reports that five terrorists trained in Libya entered the United States last weekend with plans to assassinate President Reagan or other senior Administration officials. . . .

This account, along with similar reports from ABC and *Newsweek*, began a month of charges and countercharges. The stories reminded the *New York Daily News* Washington bureau chief, Lars-Erik Nelson, of a Robert Ludlum thriller; there were even claims of two hit squads equipped with missiles that could shoot down Air Force One or destroy the president's limousine.[21] "Live and by satellite," Libyan leader Muammar el-Qaddafi appeared on "This Week with David Brinkley" to say that the president of the United States was "a liar" and "silly." Mr. Reagan retorted, "We have the evidence and he knows it." The Senate Foreign Relations Committee was called into session to be briefed by the FBI. The Senate Intelligence Committee was briefed by the CIA. The president twice convened the National Security Council. The government asked all Americans to get out of Libya and announced a ban on travel to that country. It was never clear that hit squads had actually entered the United States, FBI director William Webster said later, but the evidence deserved to have been taken seriously at the time.[22]

Where did the leak come from? The White House? The State Department? FBI? CIA? Secret Service? And why would each or any of these organizations have an interest in publicizing the information? These were questions that fascinated Washingtonians. On rival op-ed pages, two well-connected columnists tried to solve the riddle:[23]

THE USES OF PUBLICITY	THE LIBYA WEEK
by William Safire	by Joseph Kraft
New York Times,	*Washington Post,*
Decenber 10, 1981	December 10, 1981
The input from the Haig junta on the Seventh Floor of the State Department, I assume, would be to use this provocation to escalate the war of nerves with Libya. From our diplomatic point of view, publicity about the export of terrorism is desirable.	High State Department officials, when they learned of the Libyan hit squad story, were concerned that publication might upset the delicate African operation [to get Libyan troops out of Chad]. So the foreign policy logic, far from pushing for a public confrontation with Qaddafi at this time, argued that it was far better to keep mum.
Someone in intelligence must have supported that hope for secrecy, holding that publication of our knowledge of the plot would blow sources and methods.	The stories all appear to come from the intelligence-cum-law-enforcement community.
Finally, the view from the White House: . . . the case for publicity rather than secrecy is overwhelming.	President Reagan was, accordingly, enraged by the leaks.

Another *Rashomon*-in-Washington effect was churned up by a story spread across the front page of the *Washington Post* on February 14, 1982: REAGAN BACKS ACTION PLAN FOR CENTRAL AMERICA. Reporters Don Oberdorfer and Patrick E. Tyler credited "informed sources" and "reliable sources" with revealing a long list of actions that were being discussed at the highest levels of government, including "a secret $19 million plan to build a broad political opposition to the Sandinista rule in Nicaragua, and to create 'action teams' for paramilitary, political operations and intelligence-gathering in Nicaragua and elsewhere." Three syndicated columns then produced three totally different theories to explain the who and why of the supposed leak. Flora Lewis wrote about "amateur leakers" in Washington, "people whose aim is not so much to manipulate the daily course of events as to blow the whistle on abuse, deceit, wrong headedness that they have come to find intolerable and impossible to stop through government procedures." The *Post* story, she concluded, was "evidently leaked to blow a whistle."[24] Rowland Evans and Robert Novak felt there was nothing amateurish about the leak. They suspected White House operatives whose rationale was that the president would "suffer politically" if the United States intervened in Central America, and therefore they wanted to set off "a public reaction" against the plan. "The White House undermined its own plan," contended the columnists.[25] Finally, Georgie Anne Geyer suspected that the administration planted the story to use "the threat of covert warfare and activity as an overt military threat." This is why, she concluded, "the administration's 'anger' over the supposed leaks was barely halfhearted."[26] The three theories are logical, internally consistent, and interesting. But they cannot all be correct; possibly all are wrong. Strangely, when it is not their story, reporters who have themselves worked Washington's informal channels of communication often assume that a leak has a single source or a single cause or both. That assumption is most often accurate when a specific document is leaked, but this did not appear to be the case in either the Libyan hit squad or Central America covert operations stories.

REAGAN AIDES URGE INCREASE IN TAXES ON CONSUMER ITEMS
by Edward Cowan
New York Times, January 7

President Reagan's economic advisers have reached a consensus that he seek increases in "consumption taxes," including those on alcohol, tobacco and gasoline, as part of a strategy to shrink budget deficits in the next few years well below $100 billion. . . .

It was expected that the president would announce whether there would be a new tax proposal when he delivered his State of the Union message on January 26. Prospects that taxes might go up, suggested by Cowan's story as well as in an interview with Treasury Secretary Donald Regan on NBC's "Today" program, were particularly notable because of the president's long-held opposition to an increase. An explanation of the internal maneuvering within the administration was given in the *Times* on January 8 by White House reporter Steven R. Weisman:

White House officials have been working hard in recent weeks to achieve unanimity among themselves on the need for at least some tax increases in

1983 and 1984. Their assumption has been that only with a unified approach could they hope to persuade a reluctant Mr. Reagan to accept tax increases to help reduce the Federal deficit.

Larry Speakes reminded reporters that "nobody knows [what Reagan will do] except the man in the Oval Office," and the president "doesn't look with favor on new taxes." David Gergen told reporters that the president did not want to decide in a fishbowl of public attention and asked his aides to stop speculating about what he was going to do.

A lead story in the *Times* on January 21 announced that the "President's [pro-taxes] decision . . . came at a White House meeting with senior officials this afternoon." The next day Howell Raines wrote, "President Reagan appeared to be having second thoughts today," and that the *Times* story on the previous day had caused "speculation and suspicion in the Reagan inner circle as to who had leaked it." Another January 22 *Times* article, by Steven Weisman, claimed that "the President's jocularity about [the leaks] has given way to anger. That is apparently the tone he took today reading the latest reports of his approval of tax increases."[27]

President Reagan did not propose a tax increase in 1982. The stories tended to be wrong in tone even though they contained strong disclaimers, that is, they stressed that the president would probably support new excise taxes but that no decision had been made and the president did not like the idea. No one denied, however, that the articles correctly reflected the views of the majority of Reagan's top advisers at the time they were written. Columnists Evans and Novak contended that the president's aides—the White House chief of staff, the director of the Office of Management and Budget, the secretary of the treasury, and the chairman of the Council of Economic Advisers—were using the news media to pressure him in a "game of decision-by-leak."[28] If so, it was a strange strategy. The stories were not designed to rally public support. And why should Reagan have looked favorably upon more excise taxes because they had been reported in the *Times* and elsewhere? Indeed, given his irritation over leaks, the articles could have been expected to be counterproductive. They gave opponents of tax increases, such as the U.S. Chamber of Commerce, an opportunity to apply counterpressure. Miscalculations by those who leak about what they think they are accomplishing should never be underestimated, but this flurry of leaks was more likely caused by an exceptionally large number of major players in the executive branch and the Congress, all with staffs, interacting with a lot of reporters. An experienced *Times* reporter commented, "Most so-called leaks simply result from calling a source, and if I can keep him on the phone long enough, he'll say something, maybe just to get rid of me. It takes a certain skill [for an official] to say nothing, not to be afraid of being a bore."

ARMS COST COULD EXCEED PLAN
BY $750 BILLION, LEADERS TOLD

by George C. Wilson
Washington Post, January 8

Pentagon executives were warned yesterday that President Reagan's plan to rearm America, as interpreted by the Joint Chiefs of Staff, could cost up to $750 billion more than the administration has earmarked over the next five years. . . .

The warning was made "in a report presented at yesterday's [Defense Resources Board] meeting by Richard D. DeLauer, head of weapons research and procurement." The *Post's* Pentagon reporter quoted liberally from the secret report and added, "a Pentagon executive who was at the Resources Board meeting confirmed that the whole purpose of the session was to bring about greater realism in projecting how much the Pentagon can afford to buy between now and the end of the decade."

Later, when asked to investigate the Defense Department's investigation of the leak, the General Accounting Office noted that there were twenty-four principal participants at the January 7 meeting, including the deputy secretary of defense, two under secretaries of defense, the secretaries of the army, navy, and air force, and the Joint Chiefs of Staff. There were also staff members assisting in the briefing, staff members with access to the briefing books, and other staff members who were debriefed after the meeting.[29]

On the day Wilson's article appeared, Deputy Secretary Frank Carlucci initiated an investigation that, according to the GAO report, would "set a precedent with respect to the level and number of officials involved." The Pentagon's second-ranking official must have been particularly upset that the reporter was calling around to verify his information within two hours after the Defense Resources Board meeting adjourned. Carlucci volunteered to take a lie detector test to determine whether he had been the leaker and urged others to do likewise. One participant complained, "It is . . . like asking someone to volunteer for root canal work."[30] By January 12 the lie detector had been used on thirteen individuals; twenty-six people were eventually polygraphed.

Because the administration was just wrapping up the fiscal 1983 budget with a substantial increase for defense, it was more than routinely sensitive to talk of underestimated weapons costs. Secretary Weinberger promptly told

CBS that he had not "the slightest intention" of approving the higher figure. Wilson had reported "simply a wish list and nothing more."

The polygraph investigation story appeared in the *Washington Post* on January 13. Asked about what had initiated resorting to lie detectors, Henry E. Catto, assistant secretary of defense for public affairs, responded at his regular briefing on January 14, "Well, I certainly wouldn't for a minute say that the particular DRB meeting dealing with budget is likely to endanger national defense. . . . It's the principle of the thing that we strenuously object to, the expression of minority opinion via leaks to the news media designed to influence the course of events. We feel that things ought to be decided in camera and then a policy supported by everyone who stays on the team." In a later interview with Wilson, Catto added, "if you all thought that every editorial board meeting of the *Washington Post* was going to be on the front page of the *Journal* or the *Times* the next day, it would inhibit your freedom to plan and discuss what stories you're going to work on. It would be a difficult situation, and that's the situation we're in." At the same time, stories about the investigation received more attention than the story that had set off the investigation.

In April the Pentagon revealed that it had found the leaker and he would be dismissed. The accused was John C. F. Tillson, director of manpower management in the Office of the Assistant Secretary of Defense for Management. He had flunked three lie detector tests. But at this point Wilson, sixteen years on the defense beat, sent a letter to the secretary of defense: "An honorable man stands falsely accused. . . . I give you my word, John was in no way connected with the story I gathered and wrote." The Pentagon then reprimanded Tillson, whose lawyer, James Heller, was quoted in the *Post* of May 20 as saying that this was a "complete vindication, although I would rather have seen them send him a letter of apology." The subsequent GAO report said that the Defense Department had conducted sixty-eight investigations into the leaking of classified information since January 1975, and "in no case was there any indication that an individual was removed from a position of trust because of an investigation. In most cases, the sources of the leaks could not be determined because of the wide dissemination of the classified information."

On May 27, as the result of another leak, Wilson reported that a "secret Pentagon planning document makes clear that the administration has no intention of filling what in the past it has dismissed as the military's 'wish list.'" This, too, was classified information, but Secretary Weinberger apparently did not find this leak objectionable.

U.S. REPORTED TO REJECT JET SALE TO TAIWAN
by Don Oberdorfer
Washington Post, January 11

The Reagan administration, seeking to avert a falling out with the People's Republic of China, has decided against selling new high performance jet fighters to Taiwan. . . . There is no doubt that Taiwan and its backers in the United States would be sorely disappointed by the administration's decision. Ronald Reagan long had been counted as a special friend of Taiwan based on close ties before his election to the presidency.

The story on the decision not to sell jet fighters to Taiwan was cited at the White House on January 13 when Larry Speakes explained the administration's plan to crack down on leakers. "We do think it did not allow us to conduct foreign policy in an orderly manner," he told the noon briefing. "We were in the process of consulting with allies and we were in the process of consulting with members of the Congress, and this appeared in the press before this consultation process was completed."

Oberdorfer and other diplomatic correspondents had been expecting an announcement on the sale, but they did not know when. The *Post* reporter was to have had an appointment with John Holdridge, assistant secretary of state for East Asian and Pacific affairs, on Friday, January 8, which Holdridge's secretary cancelled at the last minute. Holdridge had laryngitis, she said. Unlikely, thought the reporter. On Sunday, Oberdorfer was listening to the evening news on ABC, when Jack Smith reported the decision on the Taiwan jets. "The minute I heard it I knew it was right," Oberdorfer later told me. "I was piggybacking off ABC, but since nobody in this town watches, it never happened." The *Post* reporter then started phoning until someone reacted, "My God, the President said that this one must be held close to the chest." Oberdorfer wrote the paper's lead story at his dining room table without having had to leave home.

Jack Smith says he got the initial tip on the story from another reporter who was peeved that his editor did not think it was important. Smith worked Friday and Saturday. Clearly his operation did not think much of the story either, holding it over from Saturday night to Sunday night and even then using it in the second half of the program. Smith's report was less specific than Oberdorfer's. Still, the ABC correspondent said he felt a little out on a limb and was relieved when he saw the *Post*'s front page on Monday. Smith later said, "It occurred to me to ask [his key source] whether this story endangered U.S. policy or compromised it in any way. I was told that it didn't. If the answer had been otherwise, I was prepared to make a strong case to my editor not to use the story at that time."

On January 12, at a hastily called briefing in the early evening, a spokesman delivered a statement from the president:

> Unauthorized disclosure of classified information under the jurisdiction of the National Security Council and of classified intelligence reports is a problem of major proportions within the U.S. Government. The Constitution of the United States provides for the protection of individual rights and liberties, including freedom of speech and freedom of the press, but it also requires that Government functions be discharged efficiently and effectively, especially where the national security is involved. As President of the United States, I am responsible for honoring both constitutional requirements, and I intend to do so in a balanced and careful manner. I do not believe, however, that the Constitution entitles Government employees, entrusted with confidential information critical to the functioning and effectiveness of the Government, to disclose such information with impunity. Yet this is precisely the situation we have. It must not be allowed to continue.[31]

The statement went on to establish specific policies. The president directed that "all contacts" with reporters in which classified information was to be discussed would require the "advance approval of a senior official" and must be followed by a memorandum outlining "all information provided to the media representatives." Fewer officials would have access to intelligence documents. "In the event of unauthorized disclosure," officials would be investigated and the investigations would "include the use of all legal methods." Although briefer David Gergen insisted that there had been a string of damaging national security leaks, he cited only Oberdorfer's story. However, as if to underline the administration's concern, on January 13 the *Post* ran another story by George Wilson: CRATES OF SOVIET AIRCRAFT DETECTED NEAR HAVANA. Some officials were to contend that this caused the crates to disappear suddenly and also may have revealed the accuracy of U.S. satellite cameras.

Nevertheless, the reaction from the press to Reagan's directive was swift. The head of the State Department Correspondents Association, Barrie Dunsmore, attacked it as having a chilling impact on sources. Jack Landau, executive director of the Reporters' Committee for Freedom of the Press, said he could see "no other reason for the White House to look over the shoulder of every policy maker who talks with the press except to make sure that whatever information gets out makes the administration look good."[32] Columnists and editorialists joined in the criticism.

Inside the government, press officers Gergen, Benjamin Welles (Defense), Alan Romberg (State), and Jeremiah O'Leary (NSC) argued "vehemently" with National Security Adviser William Clark against the proposed directive,

O'Leary wrote after he returned to journalism.[33] On February 2 Clark issued new procedures that White House officials said were meant to supersede the January 12 presidential order. The revision omitted any reference to the controls on interviews. It left out the threat to use "all legal methods" to pinpoint the sources of leaks. Instead it focused on that part of the original directive meant to limit the number of people with access to classified data. White House officials admitted that the new policy was now pretty much a reiteration of the old policy.

At a news conference on January 19, 1982, President Reagan declared that leaks had "reached a new high." Although the *Sporting News* does not keep administration-by-administration statistics, his claim was probably correct. This new record, some contended, resulted from the number of undisciplined ideologues that Reagan brought to Washington, the theory being that leaks rise in direct proportion to the ideological content of an administration.[34] Others argue that it comes from the president's management style: "If every policy is constantly up for a committee decision," said a *Wall Street Journal* editorial, "you are constantly inviting contending parties to fight it out through leaks to the press."[35] Still, all modern presidents, regardless of ideology or other distinguishing features, have complained bitterly about leaks,[36] and it is likely that the record of the present president will fall to each successive president as government gets bigger and more complex, as more documents are necessary to produce decisions, as more duplicating machines reproduce documents, and as more reporters look over the government's shoulder. There are no countervailing forces that will realistically shrink the information glut or the access to it.

Some reported leaks have undoubtedly endangered national security, as government claims. The number must be very small, however.[37] An evaluation of the suspected national security leaks in the brief period just reviewed is instructive:

—The leak that most infuriated the Pentagon, George Wilson's story of the possible $750 billion budget overrun, was an embarrassment to a cost-conscious administration, but even the assistant secretary of defense had to admit that it did not endanger national security.

—The presence of MIGs in Havana could hardly have been a surprise to the Soviets or the Cubans, and the United States would have to have a low opinion of Soviet intelligence operations to assume that they would be surprised to know that we knew.

—The story on covert actions planned against Nicaragua most closely resembled a consequential security leak. Yet as Georgie Anne Geyer pointed out, the administration's anger was "barely halfhearted," usually a clue that the leak was authorized. But even if that was not the case in this instance, the reaction suggests the administration concluded that the surfacing of this threat would turn out to be in the interest of what the government wished to accomplish.

—When the administration decided to clamp down on leaks of classified information, the only story cited to justify its action, Oberdorfer's report about selling jets to Taiwan, irritated the White House because of its diplomatic and political implications; it was not damaging militarily.

Reporters broadcast government secrets all the time, but secrets are produced in government by people with the authority to stamp *Secret* on documents. This has the effect (not always desired in government) of making them more valuable to reporters. Given the generally held opinion that the government is wildly excessive in what it chooses to call a secret—I even saw foreign newspaper clippings that had been classified—a more realistic security classification system, including some penalty for personnel who overclassify documents, would automatically cut down on the number of secrets that get reported in the news media.[38] Government, I would contend, is quite good at keeping its real secrets.

To say that government's informal channels of communication actively promote the public good has become a fashionable position in some quarters. "Our particular form of government wouldn't work without it," wrote historian Bruce Catton.[39] Political scientist Richard E. Neustadt argues that "leaks play . . . a vital role in the functioning of our democracy," and publisher Katharine Graham claims they are a "fundamental . . . even necessary, component of our system of government and its communications with the people."[40] Yet a case-by-case study of leaks—even this abbreviated study of a three-month period—shows that they are episodic, flaring up then dying out; they occur for a great many reasons that do not necessarily have anything to do with the public interest; they are never placed in a historical context; and they only conform to the priorities of the person doing the leaking. Neither the reporter nor the government official is thinking of democratic theory when they make their exchange.

Some leaks may promote the public good: the *Washington Post* and *New York Times* stories offered the opportunity for a full-scale debate on what should be the U.S. role in Central America. Others may injure the public good: the Libyan hit squad leaks ended up with the spectacle of the U.S. president and a minor dictator in a name-calling contest. Leaks qua leaks, then, are not an unalloyed good, although they are a means of protest that is justified for some types of dissenters who do need protection.[41]

To discuss the leaking of information as if it were a rational and necessary system of communicating among Washington players is to assume that the players to whom messages are supposedly being sent via the media understand the senders' intentions. If that were so, then regular leaks would be a useful way of communicating from one agency to another, from one individual to another within an agency, and from one branch of government to another without having messy confrontations or denials or wasted time and red tape. Sometimes things do work this way. But more often the senders are so clever or so inept as to be totally misunderstood, or else the messages get garbled in transmission. As some of the examples have illustrated, there are so many different interpretations of what is being accomplished, by whom, and for what purposes as to seriously call into question the utility and rationality of leaks as an intragovernmental means of communications.

The game, however, does give pleasure to the players. Washington infighting, it is said, is in direct proportion to what is at stake: the stakes are high, hence the leaks. But I think, rather, that the people who are most likely to come to Washington with each political administration bring with them a high talent and tolerance for intrigue. In their previous lives— whether in universities, corporations, foundations, unions, or law firms— this talent probably was manifested privately. Who cared? But political Washington provides the opportunity for public intrigue. Reporters and readers now care or should. The public ultimately learns more than it would otherwise. Public officials may even act more honorably knowing how hard it would be to keep secret a dishonorable act.

But from the point of view of the White House, leaks consistently throw off a president's timing and frame issues in a perspective that is not of his choosing. In political terms a president is fair game; in democratic terms it could be argued that a president should have the opportunity to make his case as effectively as possible, with the opposition then having the same right. In management terms, leaks or the threat of leaks may lead to hurried or conspiratorial decisionmaking. Especially in situations in which presidents have a strong desire to maintain surprise, the lesson they seem to learn in order to avoid leaks is to turn inward: involve the absolute minimum number of advisers in the formulation stage and compartmentalize so that technicians will not know how the pieces are going to be fitted together.[42] The problem, of course, as Jody Powell pointed out, is that "the damage done by leaks must be carefully balanced against the damage done by excluding people who can contribute to the decision-making process."[43]

"How do you cope with leaks?" President Reagan was asked by *U.S. News & World Report* at the end of 1981. "I've been told that you don't," he replied. "Everybody who has been around here for a while tells me it is just the nature of the place."[44] Nearly two years later, on November 23, 1983, the headline across the front page of the *Washington Post* read, REAGAN ORDERED SWEEPING FBI PROBE OF STAFF FOR SOURCE OF LEAK. So to stop leaks, presidents resort to wiretaps and lie detectors. They always fail. In a system of such breathtaking diversity, they always will. Nor is it clear that, on balance, it is in a president's best interest to stop leaks. Is a president more leaked against or leaked for? Most experienced Washington reporters would contend that the answer is obvious. Indeed, about the investigation reported on November 23, a *Post* headline concluded on December 13, JUSTICE PROBE FAILS TO DISCLOSE SOURCE OF LEAK. And in the article beneath the headline, reporter Lou Cannon quoted one White House official as saying, "there is no evidence that reporters were told anything we didn't want them to know."

CHAPTER 8

Reporter Status and Government Media Strategies

A MEETING at the FDA is convened to review procedures for a raid on manufacturers of illegal "look-alike" drugs in five states. The chief item on the agenda is to decide which reporters will be called and in what order when U.S. marshals begin seizing the drugs. Two TV networks have reporters with an interest in the story; in each case, one reporter is in Washington and the other in the field. The story can be handled equally well from either location. Press officers compare impressions of the rival claimants: one of the Washington reporters is new to the beat, and her ability is not yet clear to the group; one of the reporters from the field did an excellent job on a previous story. The press officers choose to favor the reporters from the Washington bureaus. The claims of a reporter's ability or the extent of a press officer's gratitude pale in comparison to the future usefulness that might be expected from a Washington reporter with a continuing, even if occasional, interest in an agency that wants publicity or that cannot avoid making news.

Reporters, then, are not always equally favored by officials. Nor are all government agencies equally forthcoming in dealing with the press or equally favored by reporters. The distinctions that determine preferred treatment are primarily defined by the status of the reporters and the media strategies of the agencies. Reporter status depends on location, assignment, seniority, ability, and employer. Agency media strategy is a function of the agency's importance, its perceived role in the government, and the kind of media coverage it wants.

In the long list of inequalities that determines which reporter gets more than just routine information, the most elemental—as in the look-alike drugs case—is whether the reporter is based in Washington. Press officers consider

95

Washington reporters more knowledgeable and easier to deal with than those from other parts of the country. "Reporters calling from across the country often don't understand the military," comments one lieutenant colonel in the press office at the Pentagon. "It takes longer to help them to phrase their questions, to get them to ask the question they really want to ask. Others are from the style page or something like that, and they have no idea what they're asking. You help them as best you can, but they're the most difficult to work with." The ease and inexpensiveness of long-distance telephone services mean that government press offices spend substantial amounts of time responding to these callers. Because of the difficulties involved and the probable lack of effect any such reporter's story will have in Washington, this service has lowest priority, is generally handled by career personnel rather than by political appointees, and is often considered a burden even by the career officers.

Of course, not all reporters outside Washington are considered equal, nor are all reporters in Washington considered equal; and some reporters outside Washington are more equal than some reporters in Washington. A *New York Times* reporter outside Washington may get her call returned more promptly than a *Des Moines Register* reporter in Washington, whose call is more quickly answered than a *Minneapolis Tribune* reporter phoning from Minnesota. Then, too, there is a steady stream of reporters coming to the capital for a few days, and they will rank between permanent Washington reporters and non-Washington reporters.

An advantage, and distinction, of some Washington reporters is that they are regularly heard or read by press officers and their employers. Reporters from local Washington television stations may get faster responses than network reporters from other parts of the country. Susan King, who went from ABC to Washington's channel 4, said that she received more attention after the move because busy officials do not get home in time to see the network news at 7:00 p.m. but may watch a local station's 11:00 p.m. news. Local reporters for the *Washington Post* who cover Maryland, Virginia, and the District of Columbia also may get faster responses than national correspondents for newspapers that are not seen in Washington. For instance, the public affairs director at the Department of Transportation stayed in her office until 8:45 one evening arranging a response for a story about northern Virginia rail construction funds. The story had no national implications, and even in the next day's *Post* it ran on the ninth page of the third section.

In response to my questions, John C. Becher, chief of the Defense News branch at the Pentagon, ranked his criteria for responding to reporters' requests:

Q. If reporters for the New York Times and the Milwaukee Journal ask for information on the same subject, which one would you answer first?
A. It would depend on who asks first.
Q. Assume that they ask at the same time.
A. It would depend on who has the earlier deadline.
Q. Assume that they have the same deadlines.
A. Dick Halloran [New York Times] is a regular. He's right across the hall.
Q. Assume that they're both across the hall.
A. Well, I've known Dick for a long time.

"What you must remember," says Richard Valeriani, "is that officials become proprietary about their reporters." He has just been assigned to cover national security affairs. "They will answer my calls because I'm from NBC, but they won't yet give me the same type of information that they give George Lewis [the network's Pentagon reporter]." A second level of preferment, then, is based on being a regular on the beat.

A third basis for preferment—friendship—is probably less common than is often assumed. There are reasons for reporters and press officers to feign closeness: some press officers find warmth in the reflected glory of the reporters, who are increasingly taking on celebrity status. Colonel Ronald A. Duchin, Becher's boss, recounted that when he makes speeches around the country, "they love to hear about working with Ike Pappas, John McWethy, and the others they see on TV." But Washington reporters' friends are primarily other Washington journalists.[1] Reporters and press officers live in different worlds after office hours. The social events they share tend to be of the office party variety, organized to commemorate a promotion or a retirement or a marriage, and a press officer who keeps stressing the importance of having "chemistry" with reporters clearly does not have any. Although reporters and press officers try to stay on friendly terms, it is rare that a story is given exclusively on the basis of friendship. There are exceptions, of course. The Los Angeles Times' Don Irwin notes of a colleague, "I think he went to college with Ed Meese. At the end of the day when the messages are stacked up, whose call do you think he'll return first?"

Certain types of travel will produce socializing among reporters and officials that may have a professional payoff for the press. Valeriani recalls acquaintances made while covering Henry Kissinger's Middle East shuttle diplomacy of 1973–74 and then adds, "a reason I regretted leaving [the State Department beat] is that I became friends with so many people who were then young 'lieutenants' and are now the 'colonels' and 'generals.'" On the other hand, the mob of reporters who follow a president on his overseas extravaganzas are no more intimate with top presidential aides when in Bonn than they were in Washington.

Good reporters with long tenure on a beat will have a competitive advantage because of the knowledge they have acquired and the instincts they have honed. But their insiders' contacts tend to be more ephemeral than they care to admit: beyond the usual attrition in large organizations— deaths, retirements, firings—military officers and diplomats get transferred, often to faraway places, politicians get defeated, and political appointees rarely stay long anyway. The bureaucrats who remain in an agency are not likely to be useful sources other than to reporters from specialized publications.

Is preferment also based on the perceived ideology of the reporter? Government officials may respect the knowledgeable reporter, but no official thinks that a reporter is merely a recorder through which information flows without refraction: *He has strong feelings about the drug industry. . . . She's against all food additives. . . . He asks a lot of off-the-wall questions. . . . She doesn't yet have a slant.* Or about a reporter with whom an official is not personally acquainted: "I know he's doing a story. Should I let it stand or should I call him? My problem is that I don't know where this guy is coming from." What makes a difference when officials choose between competing but otherwise equal reporters is their sense of how favorably (officials would say "fairly") they and their agencies have been treated in the past.[2] On the other hand, I was left with the impression from listening to reporters that the way they are treated by officials, especially when the reporters feel they have been personally abused, could influence their stories. A government agency never gets the press that it thinks it deserves; it almost always gets the press that it brings upon itself.

There is another basis for preferment. Of the forty-nine reporters who asked to see Transportation Secretary Lewis during the last three months of 1981, about two-thirds had their request granted. This is the sort of record that gives a cabinet officer the reputation for being exceptionally accessible. But when all requests for interviews are matched with Lewis's daily schedules, what comes sharply into focus is that a reporter's chances of success very much depended on the identity of his employer.* Requests by reporters from

*See "Documents," pp. 138–39.

large general circulation news outlets were honored, with one exception, but reporters from the specialized or trade press had only a 50 percent interview acceptance rate (five of ten), and reporters from small newspapers without a Washington bureau did not get in (four requests, four refusals). Lewis, a former Pennsylvania Republican chairman, usually found time to talk by phone with reporters from his home state. Unlike Washington reporters, they did not have to have their calls routed through Public Affairs Director Gosden. Lewis also liked to talk with certain national political reporters because, as he put it, "they're more fun."

The ultimate rule of preferment in the government/press connection is that who you are depends on who you work for. The solar system of news organizations in political Washington exhibits three rings in orbit around the central government—that is, the White House, the executive departments, and Congress.[3] The inner ring consists of only eleven organizations: three newspapers (*Washington Post, New York Times, Wall Street Journal*), two wire services (Associated Press, United Press International), three magazines (*Newsweek, Time, U.S. News & World Report*), and three television networks (ABC, CBS, NBC). Yet half of the reporters who were granted personal interviews with the secretary of transportation during the October–December period were from this inner ring; two-thirds of the secretary of state's personal interviews in 1981 were with these journalists (if one lumps together all *Time* Inc. publications). For Alexander Haig there were mandatory sessions with Hedrick Smith of the *New York Times*, Henry Grunwald of *Time*, and Greg Nokes of the Associated Press. The chief diplomat granted only one personal interview to a foreign correspondent. Although the foreign press corps in Washington is large, it is generally unseen and unfelt in terms of domestic impact. The exception is Reuters, the British wire service, which, because of the size of its staff and because it also has American subscribers, is treated by government on a par with a high-middle-ring news organization. Mexican television, and Canadian radio to a more limited degree, also have some clout because their programming drifts into the United States.

Reporters for inner-ring organizations often protest that their place of employment makes less difference than their non-inner-ring colleagues suppose.

I thought when I was with Westinghouse [Broadcasting] *that people were falling all over themselves to talk with CBS. Now I'm with CBS and maybe they respond a bit quicker, but only a bit. . . . Just because I'm from the New* York *Times and he* [a government official] *had been a* Times *reporter, he never treated me differently from anybody else or favored me with a leak. . . . Being on* [a well-known television program] *makes relatively little difference in my gathering news. Only a couple of times have people spilled their guts to me as a result of this notoriety.*

While watching government press officers at work, however, I saw services offered to inner-ring reporters that were not offered to reporters from less exalted organizations. In one case a *New York Times* reporter who could not attend a briefing was asked whether he would like a tape of the briefing delivered to him by courier. I also heard inner-ring reporters ask for favors that would have been considered presumptuous coming from other reporters. In another instance a press officer refused a *New York Times* reporter's request to have material sent by courier when it was otherwise available, and no story appeared.

The middle ring of Washington journalism is made up of major independent newspapers such as the *Chicago Tribune*, large newspaper chains like Gannett, and the Cable News Network. Inner-ring organizations automatically get a seat on the secretary of state's plane when he takes a trip abroad (along with a reporter for the government's Voice of America); middle-ring organizations scramble for a couple of undesignated seats and use whatever argument at hand to press their claim, such as being from the president's home state.[4] White House travel, on the other hand, is rarely a distinguishing characteristic between inner and middle rings because planes are usually added to fit the demand.[5] Whether news organizations assign a Washington reporter to overseas trips of a secretary of defense or cover him with their foreign correspondents are ad hoc decisions based on the cost of each trip divided by anticipated news value. The expense to news organizations of all travel with a president or cabinet members, however, is so exorbitant that it constitutes a distinguishing characteristic between the middle ring and the outer-ring—those reporters who handle primarily regional or local-angle news, who work exclusively for commercial radio and television stations, and those who represent special-pleader publications, along with free-lance writers who have not published best-sellers.[6]

The serious specialized or trade publications are in their own solar system and cultivate special relationships with the personnel of the agencies in their domain. The Food and Drug Administration only once appeared on the front pages of the *New York Times* and *Washington Post* while I was observing it, and even then the stories fell below the fold on slow days. (The Tylenol tragedy and the implanting of an artificial heart came later.) Still, for FDA Commissioner Arthur Hull Hayes, Jr., there were other clientele that needed attending to. In September and October 1981, for instance, *American*

Pharmacy published what it claimed was "the first exclusive interview with Hayes," *Drug Topics* published what it claimed was his "first official interview with a newsman," and *MD&DI* (Medical Device and Diagnostic Industry) printed a guest editorial by him. The trade press, with nicknames to insiders like "the pink sheet" and "the gray sheet," are carefully followed by government regulators and the regulated. *Food Chemical News* (at $310 a year for single-copy subscriptions) has 127 subscribers at the FDA. When calls go out to alert news organizations to a story, specialized publications account for a quarter of the Pentagon's call list and almost half of the FDA's.

The ring that a reporter's publication belongs to determines his status and the level of response he receives, tempered, as I have noted, by such other factors as longevity on a beat. Although a fledgling reporter can ask a press conference question of the secretary of state and all reporters can observe the same events, even if they cannot all sit in the front row, this is not a classless society. Cabinet officers talk with columnists who appear in inner-ring publications, press secretaries talk with middle-ring bureau chiefs, assistants to press secretaries talk with outer-ring reporters, and bureaucrats talk with trade publication editors. Not exclusively, of course, but tracking telephone logs of government officials at various levels does suggest faint outlines of channels within which information is exchanged. I suspect that some of the use of nonattributed quotations—"informed sources say"—merely reflects Washington reporters who choose not to admit that they did not get their information from very important people.

VARIATIONS in the responsiveness of press offices, however, depend on more than the status of news organizations and individual reporters. There are also institutional differences among government agencies that help determine their media strategies. Some agencies, such as those responsible for consumer protection, need attention; others may consider publicity counterproductive to their mission, as CIA director William Casey concluded when he eliminated his agency's separate press operation. Most are in-between. Note the implications about agency responsiveness that are contained even in the masthead format of the standard news release:*

> Food and Drug Administration
> Name of press officer
> Office phone number
> Home phone number

*See "Documents," pp. 126–29.

Department of Transportation
Name of press officer
Office phone number

Department of Defense
Office phone number

Department of State

Another factor in official responsiveness is the age of an administration. In the beginning the career personnel, their new bosses, and the reporters are "trying to figure out where everyone's coming from so that, in some cases, even the simplest piece of information can become incredibly difficult [for the reporters] to get," says a veteran reporter. Another period, of course, usually comes a year into the administration, when the first sustained bout of bad publicity, combined with politically damaging leaks, produces a temporary damper on information.

Government agencies also can be diagramed as a solar system that affects responsiveness. Its inner ring is the White House and the four original departments—State, War (Defense), Treasury, and Justice. All other departments and agencies, as in a schema developed by Thomas E. Cronin, constitute the outer government.[7] In general, reporters who cover the inner government are supplicants for information. In the outer government the officials are the supplicants if they wish attention. But, of course, some outer government agencies do not wish attention, which they may view as threatening to the status quo.

At the White House an interesting metamorphosis in reporter/press office relations takes place after elections. In recent years reporters have been increasingly assigned to cover the president after they covered the winning candidate (the notable exceptions are the wire services—AP, UPI, and Reuters—where there are more rigid seniority systems). Television networks, newsmagazines, and leading newspapers want their White House reporters to have special connections with presidential assistants, who are usually former campaign aides. But in a campaign the reporters and the staff are supplicants to each other. A candidate, especially in the preconvention phase, is still in competition for press attention. When a candidate becomes president, however, reporters must pay attention. Reporter/staff relations in the White House become less reciprocal.

The excesses of what government tells or fails to tell the press will most often occur when the relationship between the two institutions is most unequal—on either side: a supplicant agency may overreach to make news; a nonsupplicant agency may be overprotective of what should be news. News organizations, too, can suffer from arrogance or servility. Equals tend to have the healthiest fights and cohabitations.

Reporter/agency relations also depend on the type of news media involved. It is hardly surprising that the medium of choice for presidents has become television. Elected officials need to reach voters; diplomats, generals, and bureaucrats do not necessarily. I counted fifteen television cameras at one White House bill-signing ceremony and six cameras and twenty-seven people (mostly technicians) in the president's office for a routine photo opportunity. Because pictures dominate the planning and timing of White House events, the beat becomes less attractive to print journalists. The State and Defense departments, on the other hand, are essentially print beats. The Pentagon offers only one small room, partitioned into separate offices, for NBC, ABC, and CBS, with the CNN reporter's desk in the entryway; while talking with an NBC reporter, I could hear ABC and CBS reporters calling in their stories. "If I want privacy I go to a pay phone down the hall," one reporter commented. That the State Department now allows cameras into the daily briefings has not challenged the dominance of print on this beat; it merely gives the networks' diplomatic correspondents an extra visual angle that may help them sell a talking-heads story to their producers. With its reliance on pictures, television news is also at a disadvantage when sources insist on anonymity, almost always the case in national security affairs. Yet TV reporters have been helped by the world roving of recent secretaries of state; before John Foster Dulles, secretaries were a sedentary lot. Television also rates a higher priority at Foggy Bottom when the secretary of state is abroad, as is clear from the elaborate summaries of TV stories that headquarters cables to the traveling party—a service that is more perfunctory when the secretary of state is in Washington. As a rule of thumb, however, the more technical the work of an agency, the more specialized or "serious" the news media it favors. The deputy commissioner at the Food and Drug Administration says he takes calls only from reporters for trade and scientific publications; those from the mass media he refers to the public affairs office. But even at the FDA's public affairs office, a press officer says, "Broadcast people frighten me. I'm dealing with a stacked deck. They're performers."[8]

Each government agency's strategy toward the press, which determines the news organizations or type of medium it will favor, partly depends on the reading or listening habits of those it wishes to influence. For instance, the New York Times is considered the publication that is most circulated within embassies and foreign ministries. At least, this is what the State Department must believe, because as I followed events from the government and press sides I sometimes felt that department officials were negotiationg with *Times* reporters in much the same manner as they would with the diplomats of a sovereign nation. James Reston's interview with Alexander Haig on May 10, 1982, seemed more a meeting of potentates than a journalist questioning a foreign minister. I did not have the same impression of the State Department's relations with the other widely read paper: a Foreign Service officer praised a *Washington Post* reporter for being able to read the cables upside down on his desk as he conducted an interview—he seemed to find this enterprising, yet not really the way a gentleman should act.

There still remains among many State Department professionals what one press officer calls "the traditional nineteenth-century diplomat's view that ideally there should be no news at all." So there is within the department a sense of inevitability that, on balance, what gets published and broadcast is more likely to hinder U.S. foreign policy objectives than to help and that, therefore, the best press strategy is *damage limitation*.[9] Or as Dean Rusk told Walter Cronkite in 1966, "You're interested in the drama of the news. What we are working for is the repose of solutions. . . . Our business is, in a sense, to get foreign policy off the front page back to page 8."[10]

At the same time, a certain ambivalence toward reporters creeps into the interstice between the professional and the political ranks of diplomacy, such as the noncareer assistant secretaries of state and the president's national security adviser. Zbigniew Brzezinski, for example, attacked the press for tending "either to sensationalize or oversimplify complex issues," and in the same interview bemoaned his administration's failure "to explain [its actions] to the public and to mobilize popular support."[11] This too can be seen in the attitudes of most recent secretaries of state—with the exception of Henry Kissinger, who seemed to feel he could manipulate the press to his advantage. Most diplomatic correspondents do a fair-to-excellent imitation of Kissinger's efforts to cultivate reporters: *Your article, John, showed the best understanding*. Alexander Haig also worked hard at press relations, but I never met a reporter who thought that Haig liked reporters. This attitude of joyless obligation in dealing with the press trickled down from the seventh floor in 1982. The "chilling effect" in an agency that reporters talk about is usually nothing more than underlings' sensitivity to their bosses' attitudes toward the press.

The Pentagon's press strategy could be characterized as *educating* (others would say *selling*). With huge budgets that need congressional approval and popular support and with a steady stream of proposed weapons systems, the press officers see themselves as having a positive mission in helping to maintain the military readiness of the nation. A naval officer walks over to a reporter: *Let me educate you about.* . . . This attitude permeates the news division, a large space without partitions where reporters stand around the press officers' desks. Press officers wander in and out of the newsroom, which is across the corridor. The press office has a bank of television sets tuned to each network (with the sound off) and a board that lists deadlines: "COB [close of business] Thursdays for *Aviation Week*; 1 p.m., *Christian Science Monitor*; 6 p.m., *Los Angeles Times*." At the State Department the press officers and the reporters are also on the same floor, but on different corridors. Only three times in three months did I see a press officer in the newsroom. There are no television sets or notice of deadlines in the press office. The State Department press officers' offices have doors.

The press strategy at the White House is almost the antithesis of the State Department's, reflecting the underlying tension between these two parts of government. If most diplomats would like to produce as little stir as they could manage in an open society, the politicians from the White House want to be noticed. Although they want to make only good news, they are usually realistic enough to realize that this is not possible. Reporters also need news, although they are not necessarily partial to good news. So the White House *feeds the bears*. "A well-fed bear is a happy bear," said Andrew Glass, the Cox newspapers' bureau chief, as we left an early morning White House briefing. Jody Powell described his White House strategy as "keeping the press focused on the issues [the president's staff] wanted it to deal with and away from questions and stories they didn't particularly want to tackle."[12] Jeremiah O'Leary of the *Washington Times* recalls that since he first visited the White House as a young reporter in 1940, the press corps has "changed from a clan to a herd." With so many voracious reporters now penned up there, keeping them busy is more than a press strategy, it is almost a matter of survival. The White House press operation is used as the launching pad for whatever news from around the executive agencies might add to a president's laurels. Moreover, as the only executive unit of government staffed by politicians, the temptation to respond to any event or statement that is apt to be reported—especially on the network evening news, as Lloyd N. Cutler points out—is almost irresistible.[13]

Despite shorthand notations of press strategies at the golden triangle— limiting damage, educating/selling, feeding the bears—most government agencies would be hard pressed to point to anything as grand-sounding as a strategy. There are campaigns from time to time, alerting the public to cuts in service that would result from a lower budget or the dangers of too much sodium in the diet or the value of treasury bonds. There are also officials who want their names and faces in the news and expect their press officers to satisfy this appetite. When career personnel complain of "politicizing," it often turns out to be the "personalizing" of information that they have in mind. I suspect, however, that most executives would be satisfied with a press strategy of *no surprises*. All their press offices need do to be doing their job is provide a rudimentary early warning system and issue routine announcements.

The modesty attached to the care and feeding of the fourth estate may come as something of a surprise: studies of government/press relations have tended to focus on the White House and election campaigns that lead to government service at the top, or on memoirs by reporters and officials of the presidents-who-have-known-me variety, or reporters' stories of the exceptional—a scandal, a crisis, or a remarkable official.[14] But it needs to be noted again that only a few government agencies have newsrooms and a corps of regular reporters who spend part or most of each day inside specific buildings. Only eleven of the FDA's top nineteen officials turned out to be particularly interested in what the media was saying about them as measured by their attentiveness to the agency's excellent clipping service; one even admitted that he never read the daily clips.[15] Judging from her telephone logs, there were days in October 1981 when only one or two reporters had anything to ask the Transportation Department's public affairs director. These are the parts of government where press coverage "is sporadic at best and non-existent at worst," according to Lou Cannon,[16] and where the government likes it this way.

CHAPTER 9

Reflections on Government/Press Relations

PRESS OFFICES are like certain animals with undeservedly bad reputations. Reporters seem to feel it necessary to denigrate the services they provide, almost as if their own standing rests on the need to prove that they "skin their own skunks" (a journalist's explanation for not using research assistants).[1] Government workers are less likely to feel strongly about their agencies' press offices, but when they do, they are apt to cast them as insubstantial— a lesser order of the bureaucracy. And government political executives, in most cases, use press office personnel as technicians rather than as policy counselors.

The denigration has predictable results. As Carlton E. Spitzer, director of public information at HEW under John Gardner in the mid-1960s, observed, "Every five or six years, some editor taps a young reporter to 'do a story on government information.' The standard result is a piece that dwells on costs and ineptness and concludes that taxpayers are somehow being ripped off."[2] One reporter recently given the assignment begins his survey, "The government spends millions of dollars a year and employs thousands of public relations experts who can supply almost any kind of information, except how much it costs to supply that information."[3] Exactly. The government has been so lax in defining its public affairs functions,[4] often to disguise the costs, that press offices, which constitute only a small part of government public relations, have been lumped together with many questionable activities.[5]

As providers of information for journalists, how competent were the press offices and officers I observed? Were they efficient or wasteful? Industrious or lazy? And of even more importance in a democratic society, how honest or slanted was the information they dispensed?

If press officers are guilty of wastefulness in the conventional sense that they spend government money frivolously or that they do not put in a full day's work, then perhaps I was not a careful enough observer to see it. Most press offices have shabby, government-issued furniture and aging equipment. The Pentagon's press office, perhaps because it is the richest, seemed to take special pleasure in its unkempt appearance. As for working, more than most government offices, press offices look and sound busy—employees cradle telephones, switching from one caller to the next; photocopiers duplicate transcripts or texts of speeches; wire service tickers clatter and occasionally a television news broadcast or press conference intrudes. When the rest of a building is silent and the bureaucrats have gone home, someone is usually still in the press office. Evidence of waste may exist in places I did not look,[6] but in a year of wandering I generally saw press officers who worked hard and produced a useful product. I gained a respect that I had not expected for the humble press release; indeed, sometimes the press releases were more precise than the hurried accounts written by general assignments reporters. I saw a few press officers who were only serving time, but I do not think they were deliberately lazy. They were incompetent, not venal.

The most frequent and serious charge against press offices—that they manage, manipulate, or control the news—I found inaccurate for an almost perverse reason: they are simply not skillful enough or large enough to manipulate news. One writer's notion that press offices should be feared because they are "conduits of a carefully prepared position" and that they are tools of "a tightly knit bureaucracy" is nonsense.[7] That personnel in a government agency march in lockstep is a view that could only be held by an outsider. The view from inside a press office is that most energy seems to be devoted to trying to find out what the rest of the agency is doing (often unsuccessfully), gathering material that has been requested by reporters rather than promoting carefully prepared positions, and distributing information that is neither controversial nor especially self-serving.

Part of the notion that government overwhelms the press with its view of events comes from dividing the number of Washington reporters into the number of federal public affairs officers. Such arithmetic produces a ratio of one to two calculated one senator.[8] The conclusion, then, is that government has the personnel with which to control or manipulate information. Yet these figures are misleading; Washington press offices also respond to reporters from across the country and overseas. Even a ratio of press officers to all reporters would be meaningless, however; reporters contact many sources on each story. The government/press connection cannot be compared to a game of one-on-one.

A better case could be made that politically appointed officials—generally without consulting their press offices—attempt to manipulate the news; but as I tried to illustrate in examining leaks and other informal communications, the results smack more of confusion than conspiracy and often are merely the product of what Meg Greenfield has called "the sloppy, ebullient, gabby, exasperating nature of the society, especially of the political society."[9] It is this lack of discretion, of course, that eventually buries all presidents to their keisters. Still, there is nothing constructive they can do about it except to take more care to appoint people who are unlikely to give reporters information that works against the president's interests. Although leak-producing confrontations among the secretaries of state and defense and the national security advisers are almost part of each job description, presidents might modulate the shock waves if they paid more attention to potential personality conflicts when setting these keystone relationships of their administrations. (The 1981 trio of Haig, Weinberger, and Allen was destined to be an unstable construct even under the best of circumstances.)

When the purpose of leaks is to communicate between Washington players—officials, politicians, interest group representatives—Washington stories may be of limited value to the public. In these cases the consumers have a right to feel used by both government and press insiders, especially when reporters seem unwilling to pass along their sources' motives for revealing information.[10]

Arguments are also made that the press manages the news, usually through the choices reporters and editors make from the mound of information available to them. Thus according to the learned literature, some journalists become "gatekeepers" of information and "agenda-setters."[11] But I found that both reporters and officials tended to describe themselves as reacting to the other rather than as being initiators. The views largely depended on where they entered the loop: State Department press officers preparing guidances for the noon briefings based on stories they had just read in the morning's *Times* and *Post* saw the government as mainly reactive; reporters at the briefings asking for the department's guidances on the day's crises saw the press as mainly reactive. Both, I think, rather resent what they perceive of as the influence of the other over them.[12]

Without prompting from me, White House Press Secretary Larry Speakes and White House correspondent Andrea Mitchell on the same day complained in the same words, "They [reporters/officials] push the stories they want." Speakes gave an example of a worthy issue that the reporters had ignored; Mitchell gave an example of an event that the press office had manufactured. In these instances both were right. In other cases, although not often, a question asked at a briefing or news conference will have been suggested to the reporter by a government official: *If you ask about* X, *you will get an interesting answer.* For example, Bruce Drake of the *New York Daily News*, who was to interview President Reagan in December 1983, says "a presidential adviser" told him he "hoped the question [about hunger in America] would come up."

Who is reacting to whom—that is, who is initiating or trying to manage the news—partly depends on supply and demand. How valuable is the information? How badly does a press officer want something to appear in the news media? How badly does a reporter want a story? For instance, a press officer at the FDA tries to convince a *Washington Post* reporter that the commissioner's upcoming speech is important and therefore worthy of attention; the reporter does not buy his argument. The commissioner has made essentially the same statement earlier, the reporter later tells me; the reporter is right, the press officer later tells me.

More convoluted is the purpose of a DOT press officer's conversation with White House reporter Judy Woodruff. The president is coming to the department to give a pep talk and receive a briefing, but he will not be making hard news. The press officer wants to make sure that the reporter's expectations of the crosstown trip are in line with the modesty of the event.

At the State Department, reporters are waiting for the British ambassador during the Falklands crisis. They are behind a roped barricade outside the building. This is a conventional stakeout. Suddenly Sir Nicholas emerges. The reporters rip the restraining rope from the wall and rush toward him, shouting questions. A young press office secretary, trapped between them, gasps, "My God, I may be killed." The ambassador makes a few comments about the ·United States as "the leader of the western world and a very close ally of my country," smiles, and steps into his Silver Wraith II Rolls Royce. The reporters return to the newsroom to wait some more. A story of this magnitude is almost wall-to-wall waiting. After six hours of phoning, network correspondent Marvin Kalb reaches a source who says he will take one question. *Kalb*: "How much time until the U.S. expects the British to invade?" *Source*: ".Seven days." The reporter gets a ninety-second story on the evening news; in the next booth, his competitor also phones and waits, but he is not as fortunate.

White House correspondent Sam Donaldson is asked, "How often do you get used by the White House?"

> I get used by the White House every time they trot out a story and I put it on the air in somewhat of the form that they want it on the air. But it's a two-

way street. The President makes a speech and enunciates policy. He uses us, because he's communicating with the American people, but why not? We're here to cover his activities, and to cover his speeches, and if he enunciated a new policy, to put it on the air. So I don't feel that I'm being used in some . . . some grimy sense.[13]

Some spokesmen enjoy talking about their management of news as if they were latter-day Machiavellis, but most of their activities behind closed doors as well as in briefing rooms are merely variations of shouting good news and whispering bad news. Some, of course, are more skillful than others. They have a better feel for how to extend the life of a positive story. They have a surer touch at releasing unfavorable information in a manner that the fewest people will notice. They know when and where to shop around for a sympathetic reporter—just as a reporter with a story that he wants to do will shop around for a sympathetic editor to make the assignment. They adjust events to reporters' deadlines for maximum advantage. Reporters will even admire these skills, which fall inside a zone of acceptable conduct. But if, even accidentally, a spokesman steps beyond this zone, as was the case when Jody Powell leaked an untrue story to Loye Miller of the *Chicago Sun-Times*, the behavior becomes unacceptable—and as *Washington Post* reporter Douglas Feaver says, "we have long memories."

Organizations, including government agencies, would be sorely tempted to manage the news if they had a monopoly over the sources of information. Organizations always wish to justify their actions. They also think that their actions are correct, which in the case of government agencies means in the best interests of the people. What keeps news management in check—more than lack of manipulative skills and resources—is pluralism: "under the American system of separation of powers," Francis Rourke reminds us, "it is even possible to find the opposition entrenched within the structure of government itself."[14] And since Rourke's treatise, published in 1961, there has been a quantum jump in the number of sources of information: nongovernmental organizations, think tanks, and public-interest advocates. Walter Friedenberg of the Scripps-Howard Newspapers says that he once worried about the absence of "independent verification" when he reported on government, but now he feels surrounded by groups that are anxious to present him with competing data.

Still, most news comes from government, and if it is skillfully presented, has a significant advantage over competition. Moreover, as previously noted, most press officers and Washington reporters agree that some lies "for the public good" are justifiable in a democracy.[15] I did not see outright lying.

Press officers hedge, they insinuate, but I always felt they thought they were playing by rules that reporters understood. Press officers and reporters were honorable with each other. This may seem faint praise, however, to news readers and listeners. These consumers are not always aware of the rules and are growing less willing to trust officials' and reporters' assurances that their agreements are in the public interest.[16] Does an honest lie protect national security or merely shelter officials from embarrassment? Do conventions of attribution—background or deep background or off the record—help provide more information to the public, or do they simply make official accountability harder to pinpoint?

Most of the charges about government misinformation in recent years have stemmed from the U.S. involvement in Vietnam. One military press officer commented, "There was so much bad blood—on both sides. We briefed every day and it was hot. *It was hot.* They didn't believe anything we said." Perhaps things have changed. An experienced reporter, but not someone who had been at the Pentagon during the war, said, "Vietnam taught them that they can't have second-rate people in public affairs. These are [now] all people who could do well in other places; they're not rejects." There have also been reorganizations. Yet I doubt that changes in personnel and an improved configuration of boxes on a chart explain much. Wars are special situations. The military services close ranks; secrets become synonymous with national security. In World War I and World War II the people rallied round, led by journalists.[17] But Vietnam, the unpopular war, is more likely a harbinger of future encounters that are not on U.S. soil or in Europe. Phillip Knightley, in a brilliant account of war correspondents from the Crimea to Vietnam, resurrects a line from Senator Hiram Johnson: "The first casualty when war comes is truth." I happened to observe the government/press connection in peacetime.[18]

ASSUMING, then, that agency press operations are rarely centers of peacetime misinformation and are even competently staffed, there still remains a question of their value in a society in which there is no shortage of reporters who can search for their own stories inside governmental Washington. But it is, in fact, this very growth in the number of reporters that creates the rationale for press offices. As James Reston told Dom Bonafede of the *National Journal* in 1982, "Once you pass a certain number of people in the press corps, all the ground rules are different and the relationships are all different."[19] There are too many reporters for each of them to be able to interview the top officials of government. One solution is to consolidate interviews into briefings or press conferences and to distribute more routine material. Such functions require a logistical infrastructure, otherwise known as the press office. The other rationale is that the growth in government has outstripped the resources that a for-profit news system can dedicate to Washington coverage, and only the assistance of government, in the shape of the press office, can ensure that reporters get the basic information they need in the time allotted to them by their organizations.

I. F. Stone once wrote that there is "no other city, and no other world capital, in which life is made so easy for the newspaperman." He was referring specifically to "the advance release," "the prepared text," and "the small army of public information officers waiting in every agency to answer his queries. . . ."[20] What are the responsibilities of government to provide reporters with data? Not "Mr. Secretary, what is your position on . . . " but "how many children did Sadat have?" A State Department press officer says about the Sadat question: "I resent getting information for reporters that my son could have looked up in an encyclopedia." More significantly, the FDA press chief wonders, "should I let Faye spend hours researching a query on an obscure drug for an obscure publication?" A very good question. Faye's time costs money. To what extent should taxpayers subsidize what Arthur Okun would have called "an extra helping of information"?[21] Besides, the news industry is profitable; there are also information services for hire. Why should government aid the obviously healthy or compete with an efficient part of the private sector?

In none of the agencies I visited did I find guidelines that defined for press officer and reporter the limits of government's intended helpfulness, and this sometimes led to ill feelings. The Pentagon was an exception. Other than during the invasion of Grenada, when the government changed the rule that reporters had come to expect and banned them from the battle scene, I found fewer misunderstandings between the regulars and the press officers at the Defense Department than at other agencies. This, I think, is because Pentagon reporters and military personnel have a much clearer sense of what is off limits.[22] Reporters, for example, know that they will not get answers to questions about the presence or absence of nuclear weapons locations; operational deployments of ships, troops, and aircraft, except during exercises; or contingency operations plans. *

Only the press offices must try to abide by the fictions that all news organizations are equal and all reporters are equally talented. Politicians can

*See "Documents," p. 136.

be expected to favor the reporters and the media most important to their mission, whether it is getting elected or getting a budget authorization bill through a congressional committee. A Washington reporter for a small newspaper complains, "they [the president's assistants] provide access for important reporters *at the top* of the chain of command."[23] Presumably his access is at the bottom. In other words the desirable interviews at the White House, the quintessentially political office, go to the correspondents from CBS and *Time*, and not to his paper, the *Arkansas Gazette*. But the press offices, as relatively evenhanded dispensers of information, serve as a leveling force in what is otherwise a steeply hierarchical environment. Viewed as a government subsidy program, press operations thus tend to provide benefits that are more valuable to the smallest or the poorest or the most extreme news outlets. That these offices are more often assailed by reporters from other than elite publications may reflect reporters' frustrations over their condition rather than the quality of the services press offices provide them.

In return for having turned itself into a labyrinth that is nearly impossible for the nonspecialist reporter to traverse in the time limits imposed by daily journalism, government agrees to provide the press with a one-stop service center at each agency. The contrast between the needs of the regular reporter on a beat and those of the reporter who comes around for an occasional story can be seen most starkly at the Defense Department. For those reporters who learn to navigate the Pentagon's corridors, the very vastness of the place works to their advantage. "If someone is promoting the M-1 tank, there are plenty of people around who will tell you what's wrong with the M-1. No trouble finding them," says Richard Halloran of the *New York Times*. At an elemental level, explains another regular, David Bond of *Aerospace Daily*, reporters practice a form of triangulation, learning when "to go across the hall [career press officers] or down the hall [political executives] or to the services [army, navy, air force]." But for the outsider lost in the maze, the press office stands out like the golden arch of a fast-food restaurant—no gourmet meal, but easy to locate, affordable, and, if you know what to buy, it may even meet minimum nutritional needs.

From the government's vantage point, the press office system can also represent a significant savings. In 1978 a treasury official told me that most of his unit's time was being consumed by congressional requests for information. He said he was thinking about establishing a separate operation to handle these inquiries so that his staff could get on with the business of implementing policy. Similarly, press office staffs can be justified on the grounds of internal efficiency—fewer interruptions for the rest of the staff in an agency.

Press offices also help present information in an orderly manner. While *orderly* may be a euphemism for *controlled* in some cases, most of the time the orderly release of information serves the public's purpose as well. News outlets have finite dimensions—all information cannot be printed or broadcast each day; press offices help adjust the velocity of the flow. Obviously there is so much competition among government agencies and among news organizations that this is a crude mechanism. But, in the lingo, they try not to top their own stories.

Finally, press offices could be considered not only as a government subsidy or a government efficiency, but as an entitlement that flows from the nature of a free society and the relationship of the state to the citizen. What more natural function of government is there in a democracy than for it to make available information about how it is governing? Standing in the State Department newsroom, waiting for a daily briefing to begin, Barbara Crossette of the *New York Times* said to me, "the United States is the only country where government views dealing with the press as a duty."

Documents

THE DOCUMENTS included here are facsimiles of typical communications from the various agencies that I observed in 1981–82. In order to provide examples of more than one kind of communication from more than one agency, I have included only the first page of a news release or the transcript of a briefing. The communications are arranged as follows:

Ground Rules   *page*
    Department of State Memorandum   118

News Summaries and Clippings
    Department of Defense *Current News*   122
    Department of Defense *Radio-TV Defense Dialog*   123
    Food and Drug Administration *Daily Clipping Service* 124
    White House *News Summary*   125

Press Releases
    Food and Drug Administration   126
    Department of Transportation   127
    Department of Defense   128
    Department of State   129

White House Communications
    Schedule of the President   130
    Pool Report   131

Press Conferences
    White House Briefing Transcript   132
    Department of State Briefing Transcript   133
    Department of State Taken Questions   134
    Department of State Press Guidance List   135
    Department of Defense Briefing Book Headings   136
    Department of Defense Briefing Transcript   137

page

Interviews

Requests for Interviews with the Secretary of Transportation   138

Interviews Scheduled for the Secretary of Transportation   139

DEPARTMENT OF STATE

Washington, D.C. 20520

February 16, 1982

MEMORANDUM FOR: All Public Affairs Officers

From recent discussions with Public Affairs Officers and other Department Officers, we have discovered that considerable confusion exists regarding the ground rules for conversations with reporters, correspondents and journalists.

What exactly does "background" mean? What is "deep background"? When can one be quoted and when should one's remarks be attributed to "an Administration official"? When talking on the telephone with a journalist, what ground rules should be used?

Attached is an extract from a memorandum circulated some years ago which deals with these and other questions. I recommend it for general circulation among officers in your bureau.

Rush Taylor
Director, Office of
Press Relations

118

--"ON THE RECORD" means that you can be quoted by name
and title. As a general proposition, and with the exception
of the Department Spokesman, officers are on the record only
in speeches, Congressional testimony or in formal press conferences.

--"BACKGROUND" This is the most common basis on which to talk
to newsmen. As its name implies, the rule was developed to
permit officials to describe facts and policy more fully in
a more informal way than they can on the record. In theory,
quotes are not to be used from a background discussion on
the telephone or in the office, and the results of the conversation must be attributed to "State Department officials,"
or "US officials," or "Administration sources," or "diplomatic
sources", or anything you and the newsmen agree to by way of
identification.

The burden is on the officer to establish at the outset the
fact that the conversation is on background and the nature
of the attribution he desires.

--"DEEP BACKGROUND" This, too, is a common basis on which to
talk to newsmen. When you set this rule at the outset of a
conversation, it means that the newsman cannot give any
specific attribution to what he writes, but must couch his
story in terms of "it is understood that . . ." or "it has
been learned that . . . "

Obviously this ground rule permits you somewhat greater scope
for frankness. But it also asks the newsman to assume a
greater personal burden of responsibility for what he writes
since there is no visible source for the facts. In turn, the
officer assumes an even greater burden of moral responsibility
not to mislead or misinform the reporter.

--"OFF THE RECORD" Technically, this means that the newsman
can't use what he is told, except for such things as planning
purposes: "Off the record, the Secretary is going to New York
to give a speech on the 13th" means the reporter can't print
that news, but he can make plans to be in New York to cover
the speech. Nothing substantive should be discussed "off
the record" for the good and sufficient reason that nothing
substantive ever stays off the record

Some Do's and Don'ts. For most officers, the following
points are so commonsensical as not to bear repeating.
But enough officers have asked our guidance that they
may be helpful.

The first and most important is to be honest; we don't
have to divulge everything we know, but what we do say must
be accurate. And where we have to hold some facts back,
the sum of what we say should not give a misleading impression.

If an officer doesn't know the facts, he shouldn't talk about
the problem. The most difficult stories to clean up afterward
are those which result from uninformed guesswork. Reporters
are astute people; they generally know when they're talking
to a spongy source and they have no more respect for idle
speculation than we do in our own reporting abroad. But
in some cases they may think the man knows what he's talking
about and go with a story. If an officer doesn't want to
admit he doesn't know the facts, he can always say he's "not
in a position to talk about it."

Don't talk about somebody else's problem. Let the person in
charge handle it his way.

A surprising number of officers have asked what they should
do when a reporter asks questions about a particularly sensitive
policy problem. The answer is quite simple: tell him you just
can't talk about it for the moment. The reporter won't
necessarily sympathize, but he will respect your forthrightness--
and will certainly prefer it to a "no comment" or to wordy
evasions (which always run the risk of being misleading).

Always take or return reporter's telephone calls, even when
you know you won't be able to satisfy their questions. It's
a small courtesy, but courtesy oils this relationship as much
as others. And you may be able to spike a story that is just
plain wrong -- they can be damaging, too.

Don't forget to set the ground rules at the beginning of a
conversation with a reporter.

Dealing with S/PRS: We take a lot of officers' time, day-in,
day-out. Interestingly, those who are most ungrudging of their
time are also those who most clearly understand the impact the
press can have on the Department's business at home and abroad.
The Secretary of State and his principal Deputies are always
available to us when we need them urgently.

Apart from time, we need four things from officers in the Department:

-- We need the facts without varnish, even when (or particularly when!) they add up to a skeleton in the closet. S/PRS has a pretty good track record of discretion with sensitive information.

-- We need your guidance, formal and informal. In tricky or sensitive situations, it's almost always better to sit down and talk the matter through, since the average written guidance is generally pretty well exhausted after the third question at the noon briefing.

-- We need absolute honesty. The Department's credibility is a matter of proud record over a long period of time, but it is tested anew every day of the year. As tempting as it may be in any given situation to shave the facts a bit, there is always another office which benefits on the same day in an equally tricky situation from the fact that the newsmen believe the Department's Spokesman.

Finally, we need ideas. There are a lot of things going on which not only can -- but ought -- to be talked about if the Department is to have the kind of informed support it needs from public opinion. Your offices are closer to these "discussable issues" and we would welcome your suggestions.

In closing, S/PRS would welcome an opportunity to sit down with your officers, talk all of this through and answer their questions. If you think it helpful to do so, please let us know.

THIS PUBLICATION IS PREPARED BY THE AIR FORCE AS EXECUTIVE AGENT FOR THE DEPARTMENT OF DEFENSE TO BRING TO THE ATTENTION OF KEY DOD PERSONNEL NEWS ITEMS OF INTEREST TO THEM IN THEIR OFFICIAL CAPACITIES; IT IS NOT INTENDED TO SUBSTITUTE FOR NEWSPAPERS, PERIODICALS AND BROADCASTS AS A MEANS OF KEEPING INFORMED ABOUT THE NATURE, MEANING AND IMPACT OF NATIONAL AND INTERNATIONAL NEWS DEVELOPMENTS. USE OF THESE ARTICLES HERE, OF COURSE, DOES NOT REFLECT OFFICIAL ENDORSEMENT. FURTHER REPRODUCTION FOR PRIVATE USE OR GAIN IS SUBJECT TO THE ORIGINAL COPYRIGHT RESTRICTIONS.

NEW YORK TIMES
1 November 1981 Pg. 1

ISRAELIS PROTEST ANY U.S. SUPPORT FOR SAUDIS' PLAN

By BERNARD GWERTZMAN
Special to The New York Times

WASHINGTON, Oct. 31 — Israel has protested to the United States over recent American statements portraying a Saudi Arabian plan as containing some positive approaches toward a Middle East peace settlement, an Israeli Embassy spokesman said today.

The spokesman, Nachman Shai, said Ambassador Ephraim Evron called on Secretary of State Alexander M. Haig Jr. late yesterday afternoon to reaffirm Israel's total rejection of the eight-point plan put forward in August by Crown Prince Fahd. It calls for a Palestinian state and affirms the right of all countries in the region to live in peace.

Mr. Evron, who flew back to Israel today for consultations with his Government, also criticized the Reagan Administration for switching from an originally negative appraisal of the Fahd plan to a more positive analysis in recent days, Mr. Shai said.

Israelis See Dangers

According to the Israeli spokesman, Mr. Evron said that any show of American backing for the Saudi plan would be seen as a weakening of United States support for the Camp David accords, which Saudi Arabia has rejected, and would make it more difficult for the Israelis and Egyptians to agree on Palestinian self-rule.

Mr. Haig, the Israeli spokesman said,

ISRAELIS...Pg. 2

NEW YORK TIMES
1 November 1981 Pg. 26

Rescue Bid Cost 193 Million

WASHINGTON, Oct. 31 (AP) — The abortive effort to rescue American hostages in Iran last year cost $193 million, Pentagon officials told Congress in testimony released yesterday. A 90-man force flew into the Iranian desert on April 24, 1980, but the mission was called off after three of eight helicopters broke down. Eight men were killed when a helicopter collided with a transport plane while taking off from the desert.

WASHINGTON POST   31 October 1981 Pg. 4

Bush Warns of Forgetting Lessons of World War II

By Michael Getler
Washington Post Staff Writer

Vice President Bush charged last night that some of the young leaders of Western Europe's anti-nuclear-weapons campaign were echoing Soviet propaganda and forgetting the lessons of World War II, when lack of preparedness led to war.

Defending the need for the North Atlantic alliance to maintain its nuclear strength in Europe and to modernize with new U.S.-built Pershing II and cruise missiles, Bush warned that if there is no effective deterrent to attack, all of Western Europe will become hostage to the Soviet Union, which has massive conventional forces facing NATO's borders.

Referring to "Ban the Bomb" signs at a demonstration in London last week, Bush said: "The real question is this: if by banning the bomb in Western Europe we ensure the eventual domination of it by the Soviet Union, either by direct military conquest or by nuclear blackmail, then what do we accomplish?"

Bush's remarks were prepared for delivery before an alumni group at the Massachusetts Institute of Technology in Cambridge. A copy of his speech was made available by the White House.

Bush spoke in the aftermath of sizable anti-nuclear-weapon demonstrations recently in London, Bonn, Rome, Brussels and other allied capitals. Many of these protests had a distinctly anti-American overtone and Bush talked of the "exquisite irony" that the United States, rather than the Soviet Union, should find itself characterized by many of the sign-carriers as the major threat to world peace.

In the last decade, he charged, "the Soviets and their allies have contributed 10 million refugees to

BUSH...Pg. 4

NEW YORK TIMES
31 October 1981 Pg. 21

Conferees in Accord On $130 Billion Bill For Military Projects

WASHINGTON, Oct. 30 (AP) — Congressional conferees have agreed on a $130.7 billion military authorization bill that is close to President Reagan's request but gives Congress veto rights over the B-1 bomber and the basing arrangement for the MX missile.

Members of the Senate and House Armed Services Committees, who had met sporadically since July 23, completed their work last night, but Senator John G. Tower, chairman of the Senate panel, said staff aides were still compiling the details this afternoon.

The $130.7 billion in budget authority for spending in the fiscal 1982 and future years is about $400 million above the figure the President requested in an amended request submitted a month ago. But the bill is "right on the mark" with his call for $2 billion in cuts from his original proposal for spending in 1982 alone, Mr. Tower said.

The Senator, a Texas Republican, said that about $2 billion for the B-1 bomber and $300 million for basing the MX missile were approved, provided the Senate and the House did not pass resolutions of disapproval by Nov. 18.

Congressional Approval Expected

The B-1 and MX projects, the heart of Mr. Reagan's strategic modernization program, have been controversial, but Senator Tower said he did not believe both houses would disapprove them.

There have also been moves in Congress to make the Defense Department absorb deeper cutbacks in view of the slashing of spending on social programs. But Mr. Tower said he did not think Congress could make any more cuts in military spending if the nation was to have an adequate defense.

The Senator said the House could take up the authorization measure as early as next Wednesday and the Senate shortly thereafter. Appropriations bills to provide money for military programs

MILITARY PROJECTS...Pg.2

Helen Young, Chief, Current News Branch, 697-8765   Daniel Friedman, Assistant Chief

For special research services or distribution call Harry Zubkoff, Chief, News Clipping & Analysis Service, 695-2884

RADIO - TV
DEFENSE DIALOG

RADIO TV REPORTS INC. WASH., D.C., SUMMARIES NOT TO BE QUOTED

MONDAY, NOV. 2, 1981   [BROADCASTS OF SAT., OCT. 31/SUN., NOV. 1, 1981]

SUMMARY OF NETWORK NEWS IN THIS ISSUE

DIPLOMATIC MANEUVERING OVER USSR SUB CONTINUES: The stalemate over the Soviet submarine stranded in Swedish territorial waters continued this weekend, with the Soviet captain refusing to leave the sub and be questioned by the Swedish government. Sweden has rejected Moscow's explanation that the sub strayed off course. Reports from Doug Tunnell, CBS, and Phil Bremen and Jane Pauley, NBC.

WEINBERGER AT NAVY DOUBLE CEREMONY: Defense Secretary Caspar Weinberger presided at the keel-laying of a nuclear aircraft carrier, and Mrs. Weinberger launched a new American attack submarine in ceremonies at Newport News, Virginia. Sec. Weinberger and Presidential Counselor Edwin Meese used the occasion to emphasize the administration's commitment to rebuilding the Navy and rearming America. Reports from Ike Pappas, CBS, and Gene Pell, NBC.

NAVY'S WHALE PROGRAM PROTESTED: Phil Jones, CBS, reported that an environmental group freed a whale involved in a U.S. Navy experiment in training sea-going mammals to retrieve torpedoes.

USSR: NUCLEAR WAR MEANS WORLD WAR: Jones, CBS, reported that Soviet President Brezhnev said in an interview that if nuclear war breaks out anywhere, it could not be prevented from turning into a world war. And Sam Donaldson, ABC, reported that Brezhnev complained that the U.S. is setting pre-conditions on the U.S.-USSR nuclear arms talks, scheduled for November 10. Americans favor a new agreement between the U.S. and the Soviet Union 7 to 10, according to an NBC News poll reported by Jessica Savitch.

CALIFORNIA FIRES HIT MARINE BASE: Fires in California's San Fernando alley spread to a Marine air base in Orange Country, Savitch reported.

HUSSEIN LOOKING FOR U.S. WEAPONS: Jordan's King Hussein, in Washington on a state visit, is reported to be shopping for U.S. weapons for his country, possibly including surface-to-air missiles and F-15 fighters. Reports from Andrea Mitchell, NBC, and Jack Smith, ABC.

BEGIN UNHAPPY WITH SAUDI PEACE PLAN: Bill Seamans, ABC, reported that Israeli Prime Minister Begin rejected the eight-point Saudi plan for a Mideast peace, saying it is a plan for liquidating Israel. And Pauley, NBC, reported that Saudi Arabia responded to Begin's criticisms by saying it showed the Israelis are not really interested in peace.

PREPARED BY THE AIR FORCE (SAFAA) AS EXECUTIVE AGENT FOR THE DEPARTMENT OF DEFENSE TO BRING TO THE ATTENTION OF KEY DOD PERSONNEL MATTERS WITHIN THEIR OFFICIAL RESPONSIBILITIES.
For information regarding this publication call Mr. Harry Zubkoff, 695-2884

/.

Daily Clipping Service

FDA

PIONEERS IN CONSUMER PROTECTION

1906

75 1981

Y E A R S

FRIDAY, OCTOBER 23, 1981

FEEDSTUFFS, October 19, 1981

Opposition mounts against pending Senate food safety legislation cutting regulation

By STEVE KOPPERUD
Feedstuffs Washington Editor

WASHINGTON — Opposition to pending Senate food safety legislation heated up last week, as a consumer coalition and at least one Democrat representative called the bill "less regulation and more cancer," and a "fraud about to be perpetrated on the American people."

In question is legislation drafted last summer by food industry trade associations that attempts to revise the federal Food, Drug & Cosmetic Act, the Meat Inspection Act, the Poultry Products Inspection Act and the Egg Products Inspection Act. Calling for peer review of government findings on food safety issues, the bill also shifts the current zero risk criteria of the Delaney Clause to an "absence of significant human risk" standard.

The legislation was introduced into both the House and Senate in June. The latest attacks were directed primarily at the Senate version, S.1442 — the Food Safety Amendments of

1981 sponsored by Sen. Orrin Hatch (R., Utah).

Rep. Albert Gore Jr. (D., Tenn.), chairman of the subcommittee on investigations and oversight of the House Science & Technology Committee, told the Food Marketing Institute's (FMI) Public Affairs Conference here that the Hatch bill was "the makings of a fraud about to be perpetrated on the American people."

"I am quite concerned that . . . S.1442 . . . is a bill that would turn our strongest food protection laws . . . into a shield behind which toxic substances could hide," Gore said.

Contending he has long been an advocate of change in food safety laws to permit industry to rebut presumptions of carcinogenicity by showing that government science is flawed, Gore said the federal government must look at the emerging science of risk assessment, "to see whether or not we can introduce any new and useful concepts along these lines into law. I am still hopeful that can be done."

Gore, an American Farm Bureau member and livestock farmer, pushed strongly recently for the disclosure of sodium content in processed foods through his own sodium labeling bill.

He refuted food industry claims that the Delaney Clause remains intact in the Hatch bill. "Far from keeping the Delaney Clause in place, or even keeping the spirit of the Delaney Clause . . . this bill would drive a truck through the food safety provisions of the law," he said.

"It would set a new standard that would permit the introduction of known carcinogens into the food supply, if they presented 'no significant' risk," Gore said. "(The bill) would make it tricky and difficult to establish that significance and shift the burden."

Gore said the bill would also make it difficult for the Food & Drug Administration to operate within its congressional mandate, creating "an obstacle course, a Rube Goldberg-like series of procedural hoops through which the FDA would have to go in order to remove a cancer-causing substance from the food supply and the marketplace."

In essence, the bill goes "exactly in the wrong direction" in that it should simplify and clarify safety standards rather than complicate them, he said.

Gore said he and Rep. Henry Waxman (D., Cal.), who chairs the health

continued

HFI-40 • 443-3285

124

The White House
NEWS SUMMARY

WEDNESDAY, JUNE 23, 1982 - 6 a.m. Edition

TODAY'S HEADLINES

NATIONAL NEWS

"Hinckley Verdict Prompts Hill Attack On Insanity Defense" — John Hinckley
was committed to a mental institution Tuesday, and his lawyers and parents said
they will make no effort to seek his release until they are satisfied he is no
longer a danger to himself or society.   (Washington Post)

"2 Jurors Say They Argued For Conviction" — The jurors, Nathalia L. Brown and
Maryland T. Copelin, described Hinckley as a shrewd young man. (Washington Post)

"Reagan Is Donovan's Last Ally At White House, Aides Indicate" — WH officials
appear confident, however, that when Leon Silverman concludes his investigation,
they can persuade Reagan to go along with their belief Donovan should leave the
Administration.   (Baltimore Sun)

INTERNATIONAL NEWS

"Cease-Fire Shattered In New Shelling" — Israeli gunners shelled Syrian forces
near Lake Karoun at the southern end of the Bekaa Valley in eastern Lebanon
today, the Israeli military command said.   (UPI)

"Ex-General Named Argentine President" — Both the Argentine Navy and Air Force,
which strongly opposed Gen. Bignone's appointment, withdrew from the six-year-
old armed forces government and delegated political power to the Army.
                                                       (Washington Post)

NETWORK NEWS (Tuesday Evening)

HINCKLEY — There has been a national
uproar over the decision of not-guilty
in the Hinckley case.
(All Nets Lead)

ISRAEL — Continues to bomb Lebanon.
(CBS-3,NBC-6,ABC-2)

ECONOMY — The CPI rose by 1% in
May.
(NBC-8,CBS-4)

BUDGET — By just two votes, the House
approved a federal budget blueprint for
FY83.
(CBS-5)

NATIONAL NEWS.............A-2

INTERNATIONAL NEWS........A-6

TUESDAY NETWORK NEWS......B-1

EDITORIALS/COLUMNISTS......B-2

This Summary is prepared Monday through Friday by the White House News Summary
Staff. For complete stories or other information, please call ext. 2950

HHS NEWS

U.S. DEPARTMENT OF HEALTH AND HUMAN SERVICES

P81-14
FOR IMMEDIATE RELEASE
September 30, 1981

(Food and Drug Administration)
Chris Smith--(301) 443-3285
(Home)--(301) 946-4271

At the request of the Food and Drug Administration and the Department of Justice, U.S. marshals today seized fake pep pills and other non-prescription "look-alike" drugs at factories in New York, Illinois, Pennsylvania, Florida and Alabama, Health and Human Services Secretary Richard S. Schweiker announced today.

FDA requested the seizures in U.S. District Courts because the drugs were counterfeits of various abused prescription substances commonly sold on the street. The marshals seized both the counterfeit drugs and the equipment used in making them.

Some of the products seized are similar in size, shape, color and markings to "uppers"--amphetamine products such as Biphetamine-20 and Ionamin-30 that are often diverted to street sales. The counterfeit pills, however, usually contain a combination of non-prescription ingredients such as caffeine, phenylpropanolamine (a nasal decongestant and appetite suppressant) and ephedrine (a decongestant).

Other products seized look like "downers"--prescription sedatives such as Quaalude-300 or potent narcotic analgesics like Dilaudid. These also contain one or more non-prescription drugs such as antihistamines.

These products have been distributed nationwide through ads in campus newspapers, the mails and handbills at truck stops. Purchasers of large quantities of the counterfeits have been selling them without labeling as if they were the stronger controlled stimulants or depressants they look like.

-MORE-

126

U.S. Department of Transportation

news:

Office of Public Affairs
Washington, D.C. 20590

FOR IMMEDIATE RELEASE
Tuesday, December 8, 1981

FRA 31-81
Contact: John R. Winston
Tel: (202) 426-0881

FRA ANNOUNCES
NEW ENGLAND CONRAIL
NEGOTIATION BREAKTHROUGH

Federal Railroad Administrator Robert W. Blanchette announced today a major breakthrough in the negotiations for sale of Conrail lines in Connecticut and Rhode Island. According to Blanchette, officials of the Boston & Maine, Conrail, and the Providence & Worcester railroads have agreed in principal to accept the elements of an FRA proposal presented to the railroads last Friday, December 4.

Representatives of the three rail carriers are meeting today in the FRA's Washington headquarters to finalize the wording on a single proposal which will replace competing documents they formerly had presented to the FRA.

This final proposal must then be approved by Blanchette before he submits the document to the Special Court by the December 11 deadline as required by law.

The FRA proposal, developed by Administrator Blanchette and his staff, was an attempt to resolve the expedited supplemental transactions mandated by Section 305(f) of the Regional Rail Reorganization Act of 1973, as amended.

- more -

127

NEWS RELEASE

OFFICE OF ASSISTANT SECRETARY OF DEFENSE (PUBLIC AFFAIRS)

WASHINGTON, D.C. - 20301

PLEASE NOTE DATE

IMMEDIATE RELEASE   October 16, 1981

NO. 473-81
OXford 73189 (Copies)
OXford 75131 (Info.)

CONTRACT AWARDS BY
THE DEPARTMENT OF DEFENSE

AIR FORCE

Airlift International, Incorporated,* Miami, Florida,** is being awarded a $3,820,626 firm fixed price contract for long range international air transportation services. The Headquarters, Military Airlift Command, Scott AFB, Illinois, is the contracting activity. (F11626-81-C-0048)

General Dynamics Corporation, Fort Worth, Texas, is being awarded a $17,420,000 face value increase to a fixed price incentive firm contract to develop testing of the airborne self protection jammer system in F-16 A block. The Aeronautical Systems Division, Wright-Patterson AFB, Ohio, is the contracting activity. (F33657-76-C-0310)

Charles Stark Draper Laboratory, Incorporated, Cambridge, Mass., is being awarded a $19,965,500 cost plus fixed fee contract for MX guidance and control technical support. The Ballistic Missile Office, Norton AFB, California, is the contracting activity. (F04704-81-C-0044)

Radio Corporation of America, RCA Service Division, Camden, New Jersey,** is being awarded a $32,061,946 firm fixed price contract for operation, maintenance, and support services of 13 Alaskan Air Command aircraft warning and control stations. The Alaskan Air Command, Elmendorf AFB, Alaska, is the contracting activity. (F65517-82-C-0001)

NAVY

Comarco, Incorporated, Ridgecrest, California, is being awarded a $10,793,372.00 cost reimbursement contract to furnish engineering support, following competition in which 21 firms were solicited and 2 were received. Work is being performed for various programs at Naval Weapons Center, China Lake, California. The Naval Regional Contracting Office is the contracting activity. (N00123-82-D-8385)

Sippican Corporation, Ocean Systems, Marion, Mass., is being awarded a $4,029,200 ceiling priced order under Basic Ordering Agreement contract to furnish 11,200 SSXBT Probes, NSN 1H 5845-01-065-4485, P/N 212867 as a result of negotiations. Work will be performed in Marion, Mass. The Navy Ships Parts Control Center is the contracting activity. (N00104-80-G-0012)

-MORE-

February 24, 1982
No. 77

Joint US-Canada Statement on Transboundary Air Pollution

Representatives of the Governments of the United States and Canada met in Washington on February 24, 1982 to continue negotiations on transboundary air pollution.

The US delegation was led by Thomas M. T. Niles, Deputy Assistant Secretary of State for European Affairs. Edward G. Lee, Assistant Under Secretary for USA Affairs for the Department of External Affairs, led the Canadian delegation.

The negotiations are taking place under the 1980 US-Canada Memorandum of Intent on Transboundary Air Pollution. Formal discussions began in June 1981. This was the third negotiating session.

The Canadian delegation tabled a draft text of an agreement. The discussion also included an exchange of views on proposed General Principles sections presented by both delegations. Other subjects covered included the state of scientific knowledge and control actions taken by both countries.

Progress reports were presented by the Chairmen of the US-Canada Work Groups, which have been assembling an agreed basis of understanding on the transboundary air pollution problem. The Work Group Chairmen confirmed their intention to meet the March 31 deadline for completion of the Phase III reports.

The US and Canadian negotiators agreed that the meeting had been useful and agreed to meet again at an early date.

129

THE WHITE HOUSE

Office of the Press Secretary

FOR YOUR USE AND INFORMATION

SCHEDULE OF THE PRESIDENT

Wednesday, June 16, 1982

1:00 p.m.   RETURN TO THE WHITE HOUSE FROM HOUSTON

                 The South Grounds

                 (OPEN PRESS COVERAGE)

2:30 p.m.   MEETING WITH FOREIGN MINISTER KAMAL HASSAN ALI
                 OF EGYPT

                 The Oval Office

3:45 p.m.   MEETING WITH THE NATIONAL ASSOCIATION OF
                 BROADCASTERS

                 450 OEOB

# # #

Motorcade to Airport was routine, except for the presence of a man lying face down in the gutter a few blocks from the hotel, with blood gushing from his head. The incident was, from all appearances, unrelated to the passing motorcade.

Aboard Air Force One, Speakes said off the record that the administration does not support the overthrow of the Galtieri regime in Buenos Aires. "A stable government is what we're looking for," said Speakes. He said the White House has "not yet" taken any action to prop up the Argentine junta. Speakes declined to speculate whether the U.S. might take such action in the future.

Speakes said on the record that Reagan will address the U.N. disarmament conference at 11 a.m. Thursday. After the speech, the President will go to the U.S. Mission for brief remarks and later have lunch with Secretary General Perez de Cuellar. At 6 p.m., Reagan will attend a Fundraiser for the New York State GOP at the Sheraton hotel.

The U.N. speech, Speakes said, will be a "Fleshing Out" of Reagan's arm-reduction proposals.

There will be a briefing on the U.N. speech by a senior administration official at 4 p.m. Wednesday in the briefing room.

Speakes said the planned meeting Monday between Reagan and Prime Minister Begin still is tentative. "Hopefully, it will be arranged. . .We hope to work it out," Speakes said.

Aboard the plane, the President read his daily intelligence briefing on events in the Middle East and South Atlantic, Speakes said.

Kittle, U.S. News
& World Report

131

THE WHITE HOUSE

Office of the Press Secretary

PRESS BRIEFING
BY
LARRY SPEAKES

MR. SPEAKES: The Reuter wire has moved a story saying an American has become the first Westerner to be sentenced to public flogging in Abbu Dhabi for drinking liquor without a permit. So I want to serve notice.

Q   What was his name?

MR. SPEAKES: Michael John.

Q   Does the President approve of that?

MR. SPEAKES: Also along those same lines, today is Dean Reynolds' last day at the White House. Is here to be hooted? There he is, yes. Stand up. Dean will hopefully join us at some future date in another reincarnation.

Q   Nobody can file this veto message now, can they?

MR. SPEAKES: I guess you can if you want to.

Q   Well, why don't you announce that then, Larry? You say you can if you want to?

MR. SPEAKES: You may file the veto message, Hunt. Go get it.

Dean Reynolds' last day. Also it is Flo Taussig's birth-day, who has reached the ripe age of 24 here, right before our very eyes. (Applause.)

Q   I can't remember 24.

Q   Speech.

Q   We didn't think she would make it.

MR. SPEAKES: Now, this afternoon the President is going to spend a little time in the office and a little time at the House, and at 6:00 pm he will have a reception for the California Republican Congress-ional delegation in the Residence.

Q   Is this basically an afternoon off?

MR. SPEAKES: More or less.

Q   Why can't we have the President explaining this for us on camera?

MR. SPEAKES: He didn't wish to, as he was asked by your colleague from NBC.

Q   Is he ashamed of it?

MR. SPEAKES: No.

132

WEDNESDAY, MAY 12, 1982, 12:32 P. M.
(ON THE RECORD UNLESS OTHERWISE NOTED)

MR. FISCHER: Good afternoon. For once I have no announcements. I will be glad to take your questions.

Q   Can you bring us up to date on what the United States would like to work out on the venue for the autonomy talks?

A   There's nothing I can offer you on that today other than to reiterate what I said yesterday which is that we have remained confident that the procedural matters concerning the autonomy talks will be resolved so that they will be enabled to continue.

Q   And by procedural matters you include the site of the talks?

A   Yes. I would include the site.

Q   To follow that up, does the United States believe that some part of the talks should take place in Jerusalem?

A   We haven't taken a position on that, and I don't want to go into any great detail. But, as I say, we remain confident that these procedural matters will be resolved satisfactorily.

Q   Has there been any progress made in the Fairbanks mission on this issue? Do you know?

A   I'm not at liberty to get into the details of Ambassador Fairbanks' mission.

Q   When does Habib come back? When will he be in Washington?

A   Thursday this week he'll be in for consultations.

Q   Where is Fairbanks right now? Israel? Egypt?

Posted
April 5, 1982

TAKEN QUESTION FROM APRIL 1, 1982

ARGENTINA: AMBASSADOR'S CALL ON FOREIGN MINISTER

Q.- When Amb. Schlaudeman met with the Argentine Foreign Minister
the evening of March 31, was the topic of conversation the naval
buildup or the detainees jailed after demonstrations in Buenos
Aires?

A.= We ~~cannot~~ *will not* comment on the specific topics covered in private

diplomatic conversations.

PRESS GUIDANCE LIST

Friday, May 21, 1982

ARA	FALKLANDS	
	-- Haig ready for another try if asked	NYT 1 & 11
	-- US earmarks supplies for Brits	NYT 1
	-- UN Security Council involvement	Reuter 14
	-- New Peru peace plan	Reuter 3
	EL SALVADOR	
	-- Percy warning re land reform (H)	WSJ 5, WP 4, NYT 16
	-- 600 leftists blow up train	UPI 6
EB	AUSTRALIA: Reaction to Fraser on trade barriers, etc. (EA)	NYT 4
EA	PHILIPPINES: Illegal surveillance in US - Dept. comment?	
	(HA)	NYT 30
HA	TAIWAN: Martial law & the native Taiwanese (EA)	WP 27
AF	SOUTH AFRICA: Letter to Department re commuting 3 blacks	
	death sentences (HA)	WP 29
NEA	MOROCCO: Status of facilities agreement today	NYT 6
	IRAN-IRAQ	
	-- Israeli aid to Iran (Evans & Novak)	WP 21
	-- Egypt willing to help Iraq	WP 25
	LEBANON: Hill denies invitation to Kaddoumi	CSM 2
EUR	SPAIN: Status of bases talks	CSM 7

JUNE 9, 1981

WE DO NOT ADDRESS:

- CLASSIFIED MATTERS
- CASES IN LITIGATION
- DRAFT GAO REPORTS
- ITEMS REQUIRING PRESIDENTIAL DECISION
- ITEMS REQUIRING SECDEF DECISION
- ITEMS REQUIRING DEPSECDEF DECISION
- SPECIFIC BUDGET FIGURES/BREAKOUT OF PRESIDENT'S BUDGET
- DETAILS OF STUDIES, REPORTS, ETC., PRIOR TO ACCEPTANCE AND APPROVAL BY DEFENSE OFFICIALS.
- LEGISLATIVE ITEMS THAT REQUIRE APPEARANCE BEFORE THE CONGRESS.
- EXECUTIVE EXCHANGE OF CORRESPONDENCE
- SPECIFIC BASE CLOSURE LIST (PRIOR TO APPROVAL)
- OMB/EXECUTIVE BRANCH JUSTIFICATION CORRESPONDENCE
- PRESENCE AND ABSENCE OF NUCLEAR WEAPONS LOCATIONS, I.E., ABOARD SHIPS, AIRCRAFT, BASES, ETC.
- CONTINGENCY OPERATIONS PLANS
- HYPOTHETICAL QUESTIONS
- INTELLIGENCE/RECONNAISSANCE -- INCLUDING, OF COURSE, SATELLITES
- GOVERNMENT-TO-GOVERNMENT NEGOTIATIONS/CONTACTS
- DECISIONS REGARDING SECURITY ASSISTANCE -- WHAT GOVERNMENTS WILL RECEIVE IT AND HOW MUCH.
- OPERATIONAL DEPLOYMENTS -- SHIP, SUBMARINES, TROOP AND AIRCRAFT MOVEMENTS, EXCEPT FOR EXERCISES.
- SPECIFIC LOCATIONS OF DEPLOYED SHIPS AT SEA.
- USE OF WARSAW PACT EQUIPMENT IN COMBAT TRAINING. (AIRCRAFT ONLY)

DoD News Briefing
Tuesday, December 1, 1981, 12:00 Noon
(ASD/PA Henry E. Catto, Jr.)

All right. Any questions?

Q: Can you explain what the difference between the separate basing and the shell game is for the MX?
A: The current program, as announced by the President, has three major R&D elements. First, the continuous patrol aircraft; second, deep underground silos; and finally, ballistic missile defense. The Administration intends to explore deceptive basing of offensive missiles as an option within the BMD program. To do otherwise would exclude a highly effective tactic. For example, preferential defense which the U.S. could use to gain leverage against a Soviet threat.

To accomplish this we intend to insure an integrated and balanced defensive-offensive system which could take advantage of deceptive techniques in both offense and defense components. I want to reiterate that the multiple protective system basing mode has been cancelled and that R&D on this project will not be pursued. The MPS basing mode for the MX was not a rejection, however, of deception per se. Instead, this rejection was based on a recognition of the unfavorable economics of trying to build shelters faster than the Soviets could build more warheads to destroy the system. A key aspect of the IBM BMD long term basing R&D programs is to integrate from the start the ABM and ICBM elements together toward the objective of a more effective basing solution.

Q: What does that mean?
A: Good question. That means --

Q: You said in one breath you had abandoned the MPS and you were going to deceptive basing.
A: It certainly means that MPS has been abandoned, but the possibility continues to exist of trying to integrate deception in the ballistic missile defense program.

Q: Are there any shelters?
A: No shelters.

Q: That's essentially the statement that was prepared a couple of weeks ago.
A: Yes.

Q: Nothing has happened since?
A: Nothing has happened since.

Q: Is deceptive basing mobility or isn't it?
A: It can mean mobility of different things, perhaps of radars. We don't know precisely how it will work out but it has not been ruled out within the framework of ballistic missile defense.

Q: -- the BMD -- (inaudible)
A: Interesting thought.

Q: What you're saying is that the option of some sort of, you now call it deceptive, whatever that current jargon is, is dependent on ABM system.
A: Yes.

Q: It would not stand by itself without an ABM system?
A: That is correct.

MORE

137

Updated Nov. 9, 1981

INTERVIEW REQUEST LIST

DATE	INTERVIEWER	AFFILIATION	PHONE	TOPIC
	Godfrey Sperling	Christian Science Monitor	~~████~~	He would like Sec. Lewis to attend the "Sperling Breakfast"
	Bryce Patterson	Heavy Duty Trucking	(714) ~~████~~	Trucking and Adm. interview w/Sec.Lewis
	Julia Butler Lucian Fra	"Focus on Youth" Network	(609) ~~████~~	Interview w/Sec. Lewis (Student run station)
	David Gilman	Pete, Marwick and Mitchell (World Magazine)	(212) ~~████~~	Airline deregulation interview w/Sec. Lewis
	Mark Heuer	Cong. Bill Clinger (monthly TV program)	~~████~~	DOT Adm. policies. Sec. Lewis interview-similiar to Cong. Lott show.
	Jack Moore	Lancaster New Era	(717) ~~████~~	profile"puff" piece on Sec. Lewis.(Old friend of Sec. Rep.)
	Roy Wasserman	Haverford News	(215) ~~████~~	School Newspaper interview with Sec. Lewis.
	Ed Meadows	Fortune Magazine	(212) ~~████~~	Management behind replacing controllers-Cover entire PATCO issue. Week of Nov. 2.
	Brooke Alwyn	INN	(212) ~~████~~	Airlines and how they have been affected by PATCO.
	Seth Payne	Business Week	~~████~~	Interview on MARAD policy
	Giesla Bolte	Time Magazine		Interview request for sometime in early January

138

Updated Dec. 9 1981   SCHEDULED INTERVIEWS

DATE	TIME	INTERVIEWER	ASSOCIATION	PHONE	TYPE OF INTERVIEW
12/10	7:15- 7:25 a.m.	CNN Reporter	CNN		Live Interview in Sec. Office on PATCO.
12/10	7:35- 7;40 a.m.	David Hartman	Good Morning America		Live Interview from New York on PATCO.
12/10	7:45- 7:55 a.m.	Diane Sawyer	CBS Morning Show		Interview from Sec. Office on PATCO.
12/11	2:30- 2:45 p.m.	Rick Smith	New York Times	▆▆▆▆▆	Phone Interview on PATCO.
12/14	1:00- 1:30 p.m.	Jules Witcover		▆▆▆▆▆	
12/14	1:30- 2:00 p.m.	Art Pine	Wall Street Journal	▆▆▆▆▆	
12/16	7:30- 8:30 a.m.	Bob Novak	Evans & Novak	▆▆▆▆▆	He will have Brkfast w/Sec. and Linda.
12/16	12:30- 1:30 p.m.	John Mashek	U.S. News & World Report	▆▆▆▆▆	Press Lunch. With Sec. and Linda. There will be editors of U.S. News as well. Lunch will be at the Jockey Club.

139

Notes

Author's Note

1. Herbert Kaufman, *The Administrative Behavior of Federal Bureau Chiefs* (Brookings Institution, 1981), p. 12.
2. See Edward Jay Epstein, *News from Nowhere* (Vintage, 1973), whose main field study was at NBC in New York; and Herbert J. Gans, *Deciding What's News* (Pantheon, 1979), whose observations were also in New York at NBC, CBS, *Time*, and *Newsweek*.
3. See Stephen Hess, "The Golden Triangle: The Press at the White House, State, and Defense," *The Brookings Review*, vol. 1 (Summer 1983), pp. 14–19.
4. See Michael Baruch Grossman and Martha Joynt Kumar, *Portraying the President: The White House and the News Media* (Johns Hopkins University Press, 1981), pp. 273–98; also see Stephen Hess, *Organizing the Presidency* (Brookings Institution, 1976), pp. 15–26.
5. Steven R. Weisman, "Reagan, Annoyed by News Leaks, Tells Staff to Limit Press Relations," *New York Times*, January 11, 1983.
6. Dean Fischer, Haig's spokesman when he was in the Reagan cabinet, strongly disagrees with the reporter's assessment. "Haig was not contemptuous of the press," Fischer writes, "although I concede his aloof public manner may have left that impression. The fact is that he genuinely enjoyed talking to newsmen." Letter, Dean Fischer to the author, March 25, 1983.

Chapter 1. Carping Journalists and Incompetent Press Officers

1. George Juergens, *News from the White House* (University of Chicago Press, 1981), p. 16.
2. This is not meant to imply that government maintained a hands-off policy toward the press before the turn of this century—quite the contrary. In the earliest period of the Republic, government leaders, notably Hamilton and Jefferson, established newspapers to promote their factional views. See Richard L. Rubin, *Press, Party, and Presidency* (Norton, 1981), pp. 11–14.
3. Quoted in Edmund Morris, *The Rise of Theodore Roosevelt* (Coward, McCann & Geoghegan, 1979), p. 681. Also see Stephen Hess and Milton Kaplan, *The Ungentlemanly Art: A History of American Political Cartoons* (Macmillan, 1968), p. 130.
4. See Daniel J Boorstin, *The Image* (Atheneum, 1962), p. 13.
5. Leo C. Rosten, *The Washington Correspondents* (1936; rpt. Arno Press, 1974), p. 265.
6. See Charles L. Schultze, Edward R. Fried, Alice M. Rivlin, and Nancy H. Teeters, *Setting National Priorities: The 1973 Budget* (Brookings Institution, 1972), pp. 449–52, for a discussion of how government activities grew from building dams and giving veterans' pensions to programs directed at compensatory education and improving the quality of the environment.

7. The number of mid-level executives in the federal government almost doubled between 1961 and 1974; about half of the executives added were scientists who had some managerial responsibilities. See Hugh Heclo, *A Government of Strangers: Executive Politics in Washington* (Brookings Institution, 1977), pp. 62–63.

8. "Public Information in Government," *Management*, vol. 1 (Summer 1980), p. 9. This is a magazine published by the U.S. Office of Personnel Management.

9. "Government Spends $1 Billion on Image," *New York Times*, August 6, 1978; and "The Great American Bureaucratic Propaganda Machine," *U.S. News & World Report*, August 27, 1979, pp. 43–47. Also see John J. Fialka, "The Selling of the Government," four articles in the *Washington Star*, April 12–15, 1976; and Dom Bonafede, "The Selling of the Executive Branch—Public Information or Promotion?" *National Journal* (June 27, 1981), pp. 1153–57.

10. For example, see J. William Fulbright, *The Pentagon Propaganda Machine* (Liveright, 1970), pp. 85–86.

11. Fred Powledge, *The Engineering of Restraint: The Nixon Administration and the Press* (Public Affairs Press, 1971), p. 5.

12. See William L. Rivers, *The Other Government* (Universe, 1982), p. 98; Dale Minor, *The Information War* (Hawthorne, 1970), p. 4; and David Wise, *The Politics of Lying* (Vintage, 1973), p. 23.

13. Roger Rosenblatt, "When Journalists Die in War," *Time* (July 4, 1983), p. 74.

14. Dom Bonafede, "Uncle Sam: The Flimflam Man?" *Washington Journalism Review*, vol. 1 (April/May 1978), p. 68.

15. Ward Sinclair, "USDA Officer Produces Answers by the Bushel," *Washington Post*, December 5, 1983.

16. Marianne Means, "By All Means, Cut It Out!" King Features Syndicate, April 21, 1981.

17. The Outrage school is represented by Dale Minor and David Wise; see note 12. I think of the anecdotal school as "They call me Bill," a favorite line from the archetypal Washington memoir by Bill Lawrence, who had covered the White House for the *New York Times* and ABC. Lawrence noted, "I came to know all these men [Presidents Franklin Roosevelt through Richard Nixon] well, well enough so each of them called me 'Bill.'" See *Six Presidents, Too Many Wars* (Saturday Review Press, 1972), p. 3.

18. William J. Small, *Political Power and the Press* (Norton, 1972), p. 10.

19. An example would be Phil G. Goulding, spokesman for defense chiefs Robert MacNamara and Clark Clifford; see Goulding's *Confirm or Deny: Informing the People on National Security* (Harper & Row, 1970). The former presidential press officers who have written memoirs or other types of books that make use of their White House experience are Pierre Salinger, *With Kennedy* (Doubleday, 1966); George Reedy, *The Twilight of the Presidency* (World, 1970) and *The Presidency in Flux* (Columbia University Press, 1973); George Christian, *The President Steps Down* (Macmillan, 1970); Herbert G. Klein, *Making It Perfectly Clear* (Doubleday, 1980); Gerald F. terHorst, *Gerald Ford and the Future of the Presidency* (The Third Press, 1974); Ronald Nessen, *It Sure Looks Different from the Inside* (Playboy Press, 1978); and Jody Powell, *The Other Side of the Story* (Morrow, 1984).

20. For example, TV correspondent Daniel Schorr, who became news when he leaked a congressional committee report to the *Village Voice*, writes, "Fully aware of the irony of viewing the press for the first time from the other side of the barricade, I nevertheless shared the resentments of many who had been in the spotlight before me. . . . I began to understand what politicians and public policy advocates meant when they accused the press of being negative and trivial, oriented more to gossip than to issues." See his *Clearing the Air* (Houghton Mifflin, 1977), p. 226.

21. See Jack Gould, "TV: Dismaying Start," *New York Times*, March 23, 1961.

22. Don Smith, "Moyers Raps Newspapers as Unreliable," *Newsday* (January 12, 1966); "The White House vs. CBS," *Time* (May 3, 1982), p. 24. Also see Dorothy McCardle, "Moyers Says Press Sees Darkly Through Keyhole," *Washington Post*, February 22, 1966.

23. In addition to books already cited, see James E. Pollard, *The Presidents and the Press* (Macmillan, 1947) and *The Presidents and the Press: Truman to Johnson* (Public Affairs Press, 1964); Elmer E. Cornwell, Jr., *Presidential Leadership of Public Opinion* (Indiana University Press, 1965); and Graham V. White, *FDR and the Press* (University of Chicago, 1979). On campaigns and elections, see Thomas E. Patterson and Robert D. McClure, *The Unseeing Eye: The Myth of Television Power in National Elections* (Putnam, 1976); C. Richard Hofstetter, *Bias in the News: Network Television Coverage of the 1972 Election Campaign* (Ohio State University Press, 1976); Edwin Diamond, *Good News, Bad News* (MIT Press, 1978); Thomas E. Patterson, *The Mass Media Election: How Americans Choose Their President* (Praeger, 1980); Doris A. Graber, *Mass Media and American Politics* (Congressional Quarterly Press, 1980); and Michael J. Robinson and Margaret A. Sheehan, *Over the Wire and on TV: CBS and UPI in Campaign '80* (Russell Sage Foundation, 1983).

24. Especially Richard E. Neustadt, *Presidential Power: The Politics of Leadership, with Reflections on Johnson and Nixon* (Wiley, 1976); and James David Barber, ed., *Race for the Presidency: The Media and the Nominating Process* (Prentice-Hall, 1978).

25. Lou Cannon, "High-Risk Presidency Nears a Crossroads," *Washington Post*, January 21, 1982; and Robert G. Kaiser, "THE Star: Reagan TV Performance Leaves Democratic Politicians Gnashing," *Washington Post*, January 29, 1982.

26. See Lewis M. Helm, Ray Eldon Hiebert, Michael R. Naver, and Kenneth Rabin, eds., *Informing the People* (Longman, 1981). For an earlier collection of readings, see Ray Eldon Hiebert and Carlton E. Spitzer, eds., *The Voice of Government* (Wiley, 1968).

27. See Dan D. Nimmo, *Newsgathering in Washington: A Study in Political Communication* (Atherton, 1964). There are also several fine studies that explore similar questions on the state level, particularly Delmer D. Dunn, *Public Officials and the Press* (Addison-Wesley, 1969), about Wisconsin; and David Morgan, *The Capital Press Corps: Newsmen and the Governing of New York State* (Greenwood Press, 1978).

28. We can assume, moreover, that the margin is even wider at places without these newspapers' resources. See Leon V. Sigal, *Reporters and Officials: The Organization and Politics of Newsmaking* (D. C. Heath, 1973), p. 121.

29. Stephen Hess, *The Washington Reporters* (Brookings Institution, 1981), p. 18.

30. Since 1982 a study has been under way at Harvard's School of Government that includes surveying nearly 1,000 federal policymakers on their interactions with the press. The considerable significance of this work is that it focuses on the people who dominate the news at the political level. Known as the Revson Project, it is chaired by Jonathan Moore, director of the Institute of Politics, and directed by Martin Linsky.

Chapter 2. The Organization of Press Offices

1. Henry E. Catto, Jr., "The Other Side of the Front Page," speech prepared for delivery to the Texas Daily Newspaper Association, March 15, 1982.

2. Other restructurings of the White House press functions have been modest. Under President Reagan, for example, a separate office was created to handle out-of-town reporters. Some other presidents have also assigned an assistant press secretary to handle the needs of foreign reporters. In recent years all first ladies have had their own press secretary, and on occasion the national security adviser has had a press secretary as well.

3. The FDA processes 33,000 requests a year under the Freedom of Information Act passed

in 1966 and amended in 1974; ironically, perhaps, the most frequent users of this law are not reporters but businesses seeking information about rivals. Thus another reason for reorganizations of staff functions is that Congress mandates new services. See "How Freedom of Information Act Is Used," *New York Times*, October 5, 1981.

4. For an account of the history of presidential assistants whose responsibility has been liaison with the Jewish community, see David Silverberg, "The Quest for Access to the White House," *The Jewish Monthly* (February 1984), pp. 8–11, 32–33. For a memoir of representation for another group, see E. Frederic Morrow, *Black Man in the White House* (Coward-McCann, 1963).

5. "The Public Affairs Function in the Department of State," unpublished document, Office of the Inspector General, Department of State, May 1979.

6. Those who argue the primacy of other staff functions, such as budgeting or personnel, could make the same case. If chief executives accepted the advice of all advocates, they would be overwhelmed by the direct lines into their offices.

7. This problem of the "dotted-line" relationship on an organization chart, the line that represents the flow of responsibility without authority, is not unique to the press officer, of course. It is inherent in many staff positions, including budget and personnel officers, and can even be seen in the conflicting demands placed on government lawyers, as Donald L. Horowitz points out in *The Jurocracy* (D. C. Heath, 1977), or those placed on government doctors, as in James Gould Cozzens's World War II novel, *Guard of Honor* (1948).

8. The irony here is that the FDA press chief, whose competence was not in question, was later forced out of his job by his boss's boss. See "The Removal of Wayne L. Pines as FDA Associate Commissioner for Public Affairs—A Case Study in Killing the Messenger," unpublished staff report to John D. Dingell, Chairman, Subcommittee on Oversight and Investigations of the Committee on Energy and Commerce, U.S. House of Representatives, June 29, 1982.

9. One career employee us-against-us situation, for instance, erupted between the FDA and the National Cancer Institute over the use of experimental drugs. See Howard Kurtz, "Allegedly Withheld Drug Data: U.S. Cancer Institute Faulted," *Washington Post*, November 4, 1981.

10. However, in the case of congressional relations offices in large agencies, the decision is usually to centralize, in part because fewer people are involved than in press operations and it is thus easier to bring them together under a single roof.

11. Roy Gutman of *Newsday*, who wrote the most important article on the budget cuts, recalls, "I couldn't get anything out of the Coast Guard's press office. They were suspicious and impeded my efforts. Like some of the smaller press offices, they're pretty screwed up and couldn't even see that my story was going to be in their interest." Also see Douglas B. Feaver, "Coast Guard Wins Battle of Budget, Duties," *Washington Post*, April 13, 1982.

Chapter 3. Press Secretaries and Career Press Officers

1. Recalling the days of Cordell Hull (1933–44), former State Department spokesman Robert McCloskey said, "it was not very long ago, in an historical sense, that the secretary of state was his own spokesman." On the same point, James Reston writes, "When I started covering the State Department for *The New York Times* in 1941, Secretary of State Hull saw the journalistic 'regulars' every weekday in his office. There were about ten of us then. . . . Mr. Hull could explain his policies, often in the most vivid Tennessee mountain language, read from the diplomatic cables if he felt like it, and indicate, with full assurance that his confidences would be respected, what was on the record and what had to be off the record." See *The Artillery of the Press* (Harper & Row, 1967), p. 19.

2. Brzezinski praises Schecter in his memoirs, and then in the subtle ways of Washington he lavishes more praise on Schecter's successor, "Schecter skillfully and with humor worked in that thankless capacity for three years, bearing up cheerfully under attack and instructing me in the art of cultivating the Washington press corps. I am afraid that I was a poor student. In the last year, Jerry was seduced by private business and replaced by Alfred Friendly, Jr., a highly sophisticated journalist and Soviet expert. His style was less combative than Schecter's and his attitude more detached. . . ." See Zbigniew Brzezinski, *Power and Principle* (Farrar, Straus, Giroux, 1983), p. 78.

3. "Interview: Hodding Carter III With Philip Geyelin," *SAIS Review*, no. 1 (Winter 1981), p. 33.

4. Even this attitude represents change, however. Not many years ago most major news organizations would not rehire a reporter who had left for a stint in government, other than to defend the country in a just war. Company policy, in effect, declared that working for a peacetime government corrupted a reporter. Today there is a growing counterbelief that reporters can do a better job if they have spent some months or years (but not too many) inside the government. Those who have now returned to the news business after having been in the executive branch include William Beecher (*Boston Globe*), Patrick Buchanan (*Chicago Tribune* Syndicate), Jack Burby (*Los Angeles Times*), Hodding Carter (PBS, *Wall Street Journal*), John Chancellor (NBC), William Drummond (NPR), James Fallows (*Atlantic*), Dean Fischer (*Time*), Clayton Fritchey (*Newsday*), Leslie Gelb (*New York Times*), Rex Granum (ABC), James Greenfield (*New York Times*), Ray Jenkins (*Baltimore Sun*), Herbert Klein (*San Diego Union*), Clark Mollenhoff (*Washington Times*), John Newhouse (*New Yorker*), Jack Rosenthal (*New York Times*), Carl Rowen (Field Newspaper Syndicate), Pierre Salinger (ABC), John Scali (ABC), Eileen Shanahan (*Pittsburgh Post-Gazette*), Walter Shapiro (*Newsweek*), John Seigenthaler (Nashville *Tennessean*), Claudia Townsend (*Washington Post*), and Gerald Warren (*San Diego Union*).

5. For the backgrounds of presidential press secretaries, see William C. Spragens and Carole Ann Terwoord, *From Spokesman to Press Secretary: White House Media Operations* (University Press of America, 1980), chapters 7–11.

6. Two researchers at Boston University, A. George Gitter and Casey Coburn, also argue that women make better communicators. "Both men and women trust women more than men. So if you stick somebody in front of a crowd to tell them, for example, about Three Mile Island, your best bet is to make that person a woman. That is especially true of government agencies." See "Trustful PR Women Gain Confidence, BU Study Asserts," *New England Business* (November 2, 1981), p. 30.

7. Quoted in "Public Information in Government: Some Contrasting Views," *Management* (published by the U.S. Office of Personnel Management), vol. 1 (Summer 1980), p. 11.

8. In published form, the best case for the State Department's press conventions has been made by John H. Trattner, Secretary Muskie's spokesman, in "Some Notes on Background," *Foreign Service Journal*, vol. 59 (July/August 1982), pp. 28–33.

9. "The Return of the Press Secretaries," *New York Times*, April 29, 1982.

10. Lois Romano, "The Truth . . . and How to Avoid It," *Washington Post*, October 28, 1983.

11. These examples are given by Sissela Bok in *Lying: Moral Choice in Public and Private Life* (Vintage, 1979), p. 187.

12. Quoted in Leon V. Sigal, *Reporters and Officials* (D. C. Heath, 1973), p. 131.

13. Letter, Jerry W. Friedheim to the author, March 18, 1983.

14. Herbert Kaufman, *The Administrative Behavior of Federal Bureau Chiefs* (Brookings Institution, 1981), pp. 72–73.

15. George E. Reedy, *The Twilight of the Presidency* (World, 1970), p.118.

16. See Henry F. Graff, *The Tuesday Cabinet: Deliberation and Decision on Peace and War under Lyndon B. Johnson* (Prentice-Hall, 1970).

17. See John H. Kessel, "The Structures of the Carter White House," *American Journal of Political Science*, vol. 27 (August 1983), p. 449.

18. The degree to which Hagerty was kept informed by Eisenhower in 1954–55 can be seen in Robert H. Ferrell, ed., *The Diary of James C. Hagerty* (Indiana University Press, 1983); on the term "news management," coined by James Reston, see Michael Schudson, *Discovering the News: A Social History of American Newspapers* (Basic Books, 1978), p. 170.

19. This is not just a press office phenomenon, of course. See Joel D. Aberbach and Bert A. Rockman, "Clashing Beliefs Within the Executive Branch: The Nixon Administration Bureaucracy," *American Political Science Review*, vol. 70 (June 1976), pp. 466–67.

20. The memorandum from Herbert W. Klotz, dated April 12, 1961, was reproduced in a Republican National Committee publication, *Battle Line*, April 26, 1961.

21. See "Recipient of Artificial Heart Is Given a Human One," *New York Times*, July 27, 1981; and "The Artificial Heart is Here," *Life* (September 1981).

22. The chief spokesman of the Federal Bureau of Investigation during this period was Roger S. Young, a graduate of Dartmouth College and the University of Pennsylvania Law School; Young, however, was a professional FBI agent, not a professional press officer.

23. Almost half of the Washington reporters have done some graduate work, and a third have graduate degrees. See Stephen Hess, *The Washington Reporters* (Brookings Institution, 1982), p. 165. Also see Robert B. Sims, *The Pentagon Reporters* (National Defense University Press), pp. 142–43.

24. The same can be said of journalists. A national survey shows that "fewer than a third (31.1 percent) endorsed professional training in journalism." See John W. C. Johnstone, Edward J. Slawski, and William W. Bowman, *The News People: A Sociological Portrait of American Journalists and Their Work* (University of Illinois Press, 1976), p. 41.

25. Bullying, on the other hand, says a very good reporter who engages in the practice, is not a personality defect but a deliberate strategy to counter the built-in inertia of government. There are also reporters who complain about the incivility of some higher-ranking government officials.

26. See Marjorie Ogilvy-Webb, *The Government Explains: A Study of the Information Services* (London: George Allen and Unwin, 1965), p. 185.

27. There are also differences among the armed services' personnel systems as they relate to press officers. Officers in the navy and air force spend their entire careers on a public affairs track, while army officers alternate assignments between public affairs and another specialty. Army public affairs officers contend that their system gives them a broader understanding of military operations; navy and air force officers in public affairs think that the advantage of their system is that they compete against each other for promotion and are not unfairly disadvantaged as they might be if selection boards were to choose between a press officer and one with line responsibility.

28. Letter, Kate Semerad to the author, August 17, 1983.

29. According to the *1983 Report of the United States Advisory Commission on Public Diplomacy*, p. 35, "USIA's officers constitute approximately 19 percent of the career Foreign Service. . . . Currently there are 84 State officers in ambassadorial positions and 128 DCMs [Deputy Chiefs of Mission]. Two USIA officers are presently assigned as ambassadors, Three are DCMs."

30. If government career elites and Washington reporters both feel superior to press officers, how do they feel about each other? It seems to depend on a variety of factors. For example, reporters' relations with Foreign Service officers can be markedly different at home and abroad: distant when in Washington, yet quite close when they are stationed overseas,

especially in unfriendly territory. Political executives and reporters, on the other hand, usually view each other as equals after accounting for relative rank in their organizations and the relative prestige of those organizations.

31. Richard A. Merrill, "Saccharin: A Regulator's View," in Robert W. Crandall and Lester B. Lave, eds., *The Scientific Basis of Health and Safety Regulation* (Brookings Institution, 1981), p. 160.

32. Robert Reinhold, "Frantic Team Effort Brought Vital Chemical to the Stricken Plant," *New York Times*, April 4, 1979.

33. However, this is changing; Robert B. Sims points out that "younger members of the [press] group tend not to have had military service"; see his *The Pentagon Reporters*, pp. 143, 147.

34. For example, a state Department transcript of Alexander Haig being interviewed by Ina Ginsburg, May 11, 1982, for *Interview Magazine*, quotes the then secretary of state as saying, "even if they [the reporters] write something that I think is terribly untrue, I don't consider that it was a writer who did it. It's always someone who gave that writer that information."

35. The same phenomena have been observed in Great Britain, where a former cabinet ministry press chief wrote, "The majority of Civil Servants have a horror of journalists. They imagine anything they say to the Press will be misquoted wildly. Journalists usually think Civil Servants are reactionary red tape-bound creatures." See Richard Williams-Thompson, *Was I Really Necessary?* (London: World's Press News, 1951), p. 21.

36. The poll taker notes that the press information officers "showed discomfort" in such replies as "Yes, but on a 'background' basis" and "Yes (sometimes)." As would be expected, all ten reporters who were asked the same question answered affirmatively. See Donald C. McLearn, "The Credibility of HEW's Public Information Channel as Perceived by HEW Public Information Officers and Reporters" (M.A. thesis, University of Florida, 1979), p. 26.

Chapter 4. Routine Activities

1. *Wall Street Journal* Marketing Services Department, *Opinion Leaders*, vol. 1 (Dow Jones, 1979), p. 17.

2. William Safire, *Before the Fall* (Doubleday, 1975), plates 14 and 15.

3. This is not meant to imply that the Pentagon clips play down the *Times* and *Post*; on the contrary, these papers are uniquely important to this department. Another unintended consequence of the Pentagon's clipping service is that it helps to produce a better-informed press corps by providing the reporters on the beat with what amounts to a reader's digest of the best writing on defense matters, including selections from the trade press and even the so-called learned journals. Much of this material would have otherwise escaped the reporters' attention, if only because these publications are expensive and news media operations have limited library facilities. The daily clips, of course, are meant to provide government officials with a report of what the press is saying; government feels no responsibility to provide reporters with a report of what other reporters are saying.

4. Robert Burkhardt, "Massive Aviation Tax Increases Expected," *Journal of Commerce*, January 29, 1982.

5. See L. John Martin, "Government and the News Media," in Dan D. Nimmo and Keith R. Sanders, eds., *Handbook of Political Communication* (Sage, 1981), p. 449.

6. For the contrary view, see Dan D. Nimmo, *Newsgathering in Washington* (Atherton, 1964), pp. 149–51, a study that interviewed thirty-five Washington reporters in 1961 and concludes, "Rare was the newsman who found much to praise in the 'handout' as a tool of newsgathering." Nimmo also writes that "reporters see the news release as a device by

which government tries to peddle to the correspondent rather than aid him," and "the primary criticism leveled against it was that the news release is simply an instrument of governmental publicity, of utility to government but not to the press."

7. When I analyzed congressional press coverage for a week in April, 1978, there were 179 open committee or subcommittee sessions that heard witnesses. See *The Washington Reporters* (Brookings Institution, 1982), p. 105.

8. The network time segments come from *Television News Index and Abstract*, published by Vanderbilt University's Television News Archives.

9. Sara J. Fritz, then a White House correspondent for *U.S. News & World Report*, accidentally discovered in 1981 that a Katherine Burdman was impersonating her in telephone interviews. The articles appeared in *American Labor Beacon* and *Executive Intelligence Review*, Lyndon LaRouche publications. Fritz and *U.S.News* sued in U.S. District Court and were granted a permanent injunction barring LaRouche's organizations from using the *U.S. News* name or impersonating its reporters.

Chapter 5. Reactions to Crises

1. This proved to be correct. See John Burgess, "Pilot Error Probable Cause Of D.C. Crash, Report Says," *Washington Post*, August 11, 1982.

2. For other discussions of accidental news, see Harvey Molotch and Marilyn Lester, "News as Purposive Behavior: On the Strategic Use of Routine Events, Accidents, and Scandals," *American Sociological Review*, vol. 39 (February, 1974), pp. 101–12; and "Accidental News: The Great Oil Spill as Local Occurrence and National Event," *American Journal of Sociology*, vol. 81 (September, 1975), pp. 235–60.

3. See Patrick E. Tyler, "The Making of an Invasion: Chronology of the Planning," *Washington Post*, October 31, 1983; and as revised by Don Oberdorfer, "Reagan Sought to End Cuban 'Intervention,'" *Washington Post*, November 6, 1983.

4. According to one account, "Larry Speakes was not briefed on plans for Grenada until 30 minutes before the invasion." See Jack Nelson, "Reagan's Anti-Press Campaign," *Los Angeles Times*, December 18, 1983.

5. Government's responsibility for the safety of reporters and the constitutional guarantee of freedom of the press under the First Amendment were not at issue despite various statements by officials and journalists. See Henry E. Catto, Jr., "Dateline Grenada: The Media and the Military Go at It," *Washington Post*, October 30, 1983.

6. See Rich Jaroslovsky, "Reagan Press Aide Quits Amid Dispute Over False Reports on Grenada Invasion," *Wall Street Journal*, November 1, 1983. David Gergen, White House director of communications, announced his resignation on December 8 but did not claim that his decision was related to Grenada.

7. The question of whether honest lying was necessary in the case of the Grenada invasion partly depends on the degree to which the invasion was a surprise. For example, on November 1, 1983, John Burgess wrote, "Jamaican Prime Minister Edward Seaga said at a rally in Jamaica today that a third country had leaked word of the invasion plans to [Grenadan General Hudson] Austin's government a few days before the attack, allowing Grenadan and Cuban forces on the island to bolster their defenses." See "Red Cross Sends Plane to Barbados for Injured Cubans," *Washington Post*, November 1, 1983.

8. Pierre Salinger, *With Kennedy* (Doubleday, 1966), pp. 145, 255.

9. Richard Halloran, "Military Influence Is Seen Expanding," *New York Times*, November 2, 1983; also see Gerald F. Seib, "No More 'Micromanagement' of the Military," *Wall Street Journal*, November 8, 1983.

10. See John E. Murray, "Journalists in the Press of Battle," letter to the editor, *Wall Street Journal*, November 4, 1983.
11. Henry Grunwald, "Trying to Censor Reality," *Time* (November 7, 1983), p. 102.
12. Michael Schudson, *Discovering the News: A Social History of American Newspapers* (Basic Books, 1978), p. 164.
13. See David Burnham, "Curbs on Grenada News Coverage Criticized in House Hearing," *New York Times*, November 3, 1983.
14. James Reston, "How Reagan Does It," *New York Times*, November 9, 1983. Also see Haynes Johnson, "News," *Washington Post*, October 30, 1983; and Daniel Schorr, "Invasion Deepens the Crisis of the Public Vs. the Press," *Los Angeles Times*, November 1, 1983.
15. Vermont Royster, "Grenada Fallout," *Wall Street Journal*, November 16, 1983.
16. Equally noteworthy was that the U.S. government was not able to keep all reporters off the island. Seven journalists, including reporters from *Time*, the *Washington Post*, the *Miami Herald*, and *Newsday*, anticipated the invasion and reached Grenada in a rented fishing town boat before the marines landed. See Edward Cody, "The Day War Roared into St. George's Picture-Book Harbor," *Washington Post*, October 28, 1983; and Bernard Diederich, "Images from an Unlikely War," *Time* (November 7, 1983), pp. 30–31.
17. See David M. Cooney, "The Media and the Military," letter to the editor, *Washington Post*, November 15, 1983.
18. Robert J. McCloskey, "Invasion and Evasion," *Washington Post*, October 28, 1983.

Chapter 6. Briefings

1. These reading habits of the press officers were as of April 1982. Taylor later said that he had added the *Washington Times*, the *New York Daily News*, and *USA Today* to his reading list.
2. There are modest differences between a briefing and a news conference. A briefing can be on background or even off the record; a news conference is always on the record. Primarily, however, the difference is in the rank of the person answering questions: the president holds a news conference; the president's press secretary holds a briefing.
3. Letter, Jerry W. Friedheim to the author, August 1, 1983.
4. Part of what is lost is the identity of the questioner. In the false egalitarianism of the briefing room, participants call each other by first names, but there are several Bernies, Jims, and Johns, and which Jim is being addressed may make a difference in how a question is answered.
5. Russell Baker writes, "The State Department reporter quickly learns to talk like a fuddy-duddy and to look grave, important, and inscrutable. The Pentagon man always seems to have just come in off maneuvers. The Capitol reporter eschews the raucous spirit of the White House and affects the hooded expression of the man privy to many important deals." See his *An American in Washington* (Knopf, 1961), p. 198.
6. During the period I attended State Department briefings, the largest number of foreign correspondents present were from Latin America and the Middle East. I do not know whether the type of participation by the foreign press corps would have been different had the world's most troubled areas been elsewhere.
7. I was told by a number of officials and reporters who have attended White House and State Department briefings over the years that the right-wingers with press credentials are more in attendance during Democratic administrations and the left-wingers come out to ask questions when there is a Republican administration.

8. Jim Anderson, "Administration of Silence," *Foreign Service Journal*, vol. 59 (July/August 1982), p. 22.

Chapter 7. Leaks and Other Informal Communications

1. Michael deCourcy Hinds and Warren Weaver, Jr., "What He Meant Was . . . , " *New York Times*, August 8, 1983.
2. George E. Reedy, *The Twilight of the Presidency* (World, 1970), p. 110.
3. David S. Broder, "Aid Shift to States Reported," *Washington Post*, January 19, 1982. For empirical evidence of the extent to which information about the president and the executive branch is funneled through Capitol Hill sources to the news media, see Stephen Hess, *The Washington Reporters* (Brookings Institution, 1982), p. 99.
4. Discussing leaks with Laurence Barrett of *Time* in late December, 1981, President Reagan said, "there are large layers of the bureaucracy that you cannot change, and there are many of them, I suppose, who are resentful and do not agree with what it is you are trying to do. Now maybe they are the ones that are the principal sources of the leaks." Barrett then wrote, "Reagan indicated that he knew better. . . . He knew that his own people had interests to defend and axes to grind." See Barrett's *Gambling with History: Reagan in the White House* (Doubleday, 1983), p. 430.
5. James Reston, *The Artillery of the Press* (Harper & Row, 1967), p. 66.
6. Tom Wicker, "Leak On, O Ship of State!" *New York Times*, January 26, 1982. For the contrary view, see William S. White, "Trying to Find the Shape—If Any—of the News in Washington," *Harper's* (August 1958), p. 79. White writes, "the leak or exclusive story is rarely an example of a reporter's persistence and skill."
7. Quoted in Robert J. McCloskey, "How Not to Stop Leaks," *Washington Post*, February 1, 1982.
8. Stewart Alsop, *The Center: People and Power in Political Washington* (Popular Library, 1968), p. 174.
9. For a more elaborate explanation of why information is leaked, see Morton H. Halperin, with Priscilla Clapp and Arnold Kanter, *Bureaucratic Politics & Foreign Policy* (Brookings Institution, 1974), pp. 176–89.
10. Hugh Heclo, *A Government of Strangers* (Brookings Institution, 1977), p. 226.
11. Robert J. McCloskey, "State's Villainous Leaker," *Washington Post*, March 2, 1982.
12. See Robert J. McCloskey, "Publishing Rumors," *Washington Post*, March 25, 1983.
13. Leslie H. Gelb, "Dissecting a Vintage Example of a Political Rumor," *New York Times*, November 3, 1981.
14. Don Oberdorfer and Martin Schram, "Haig Believes a Reagan Aide Is Campaigning Against Him," *Washington Post*, November 4, 1981.
15. Howell Raines, "Reagan Cuts Off Haig Dispute," *New York Times*, November 6, 1981.
16. William Safire, "Who's Blowing Smoke?" *New York Times*, November 8, 1981.
17. " . . . and Washington's 'Guerrilla War,'" *Chicago Tribune*, November 5, 1981.
18. William Greider, "Reporters and Their Sources," *The Washington Monthly* (October 1982), p. 17, adapted from his book, *The Education of David Stockman and Other Americans* (Dutton, 1982).
19. Ibid., p. 14.
20. Adam Clymer, "Q&A: Lyn Nofziger," *New York Times*, December 2, 1981.
21. Lars-Erik Nelson, "The Khadafy Plot: Fact, Fiction and Fear," *New York Daily News*, December 9, 1981.
22. William Chapman, "FBI Chief Unhappy Over Publicity About Libyan Death Squad," *Washington Post*, January 4, 1982. Jack Anderson speculated that the hit-squad story was

the result of the CIA's being "played for a sucker by its own 'disinformation' campaign directed at Qaddafi" (*Washington Post*, January 7, 1982); William Safire later contended that "P.L.O. double agents sold our C.I.A. a phony tale of a Libyan hit team" (*New York Times*, December 15, 1983).

23. Safire writes that he had "no other inside information, and [was] speculating purely on the basis of institutional responses in the past."

24. Flora Lewis, "Leaks and Stories," *New York Times*, March 14, 1982.

25. Rowland Evans and Robert Novak, "Suspicions on a Leak," *Washington Post*, March 19, 1982.

26. Georgie Anne Geyer, "Covert Action: A Plus for Central America?" *Washington Times* (prototype edition), March 23, 1982.

27. See "Aides Say Reagan Will Ask Congress for Excise Tax Rise," *New York Times*, January 21, 1982; Howell Raines, "Reagan Seems to be Wavering on Excise Taxes," *New York Times*, January 22, 1982; and Steven R. Weisman, "To Increase or Not to Increase Taxes," *New York Times*, January 22, 1982.

28. Rowland Evans and Robert Novak, "GOP Defense Cutters," *Washington Post*, February 1, 1982.

29. Letter, William J. Anderson, Director, General Government Division, U.S. General Accounting Office, to Jack Brooks, Chairman, Subcommitee on Legislative and National Security, Committee on Government Operations, U.S. House of Representatives, October 7, 1982.

30. "Leak Detection," *Aviation Week*, January 18, 1982, p. 15.

31. "Protection of Classified National Security Council and Intelligence Information," *Weekly Compilation of Presidential Documents*, vol. 18 (January 1982), pp. 24–25.

32. Michael Getler, "Restrictions Protested by Reporters," *Washington Post*, January 22, 1982.

33. Jeremiah O'Leary, "Working in the White House—A Journalist's Account," *Washington Times*, May 14, 1982.

34. See Philip Geyelin, "Stop That Leak!" *Washington Post*, February 9, 1982.

35. "Who's Talking," *Wall Street Journal*, January 18, 1982.

36. For a compilation of quotations from Truman through Carter, see Joel Garreau, "Up to Their Keisters in Leaks," *Washington Post*, January 16, 1983.

37. See Harvey G. Zeidenstein, "White House Perceptions of News Media Bias," *Presidential Studies Quarterly*, vol. 13 (Summer 1983), pp. 346–47; and Douglass Cater, *Power in Washington* (Vintage, 1964), p. 234.

38. See William V. Kennedy, "There Are No More Secrets," *Christian Science Monitor*, January 11, 1982.

39. Quoted in Douglass Cater, *The Fourth Branch of Government* (Vintage, 1959), p. 137.

40. Richard E. Neustadt, quoted in William Safire, *Safire's Political Dictionary* (Ballantine, 1980), p. 369; and Katharine Graham, "The Press Can Do a Better Job," *Editor & Publisher* (November 19, 1983), p. 42.

41. See David Halberstam, "The Press in Vietnam and El Salvador," *Wall Street Journal*, February 23, 1982.

42. Chester E. Finn, Jr., explains how this happened in the formulation of President Nixon's domestic proposals. See his *Education and the Presidency* (D. C. Heath, 1977), p. 6.

43. Jody Powell, "Leaks: Whys and Wherefores," *Washington Post*, February 7, 1982.

44. "The President Sums Up His First Year in Office," *U.S. News & World Report* (December 29, 1981), p. 26.

Chapter 8. Reporter Status and Government Media Strategies

1. Stephen Hess, *The Washington Reporters* (Brookings Institution, 1982), p. 152. However, this is not the case outside Washington where 74 percent of U.S. journalists say they have

an equal number of journalist and nonjournalist friends. See Richard G. Gray and G. Cleveland Wilhoit, "Portrait of the U.S. Journalist, 1982–83," paper presented to the American Society of Newspaper Editors convention, Denver, Colorado, May 9, 1983.

2. See Montague Kern, Patricia W. Levering, and Ralph B. Levering, *The Kennedy Crises: The Press, the Presidency, and Foreign Policy* (University of North Carolina Press, 1983), p. 198.

3. Hess, *The Washington Reporters*, chapter 2, especially pp. 24–28.

4. For an example of how middle-ring organizations are treated, see John P. Wallach, " 'I'll Give It to You on Background': State Breakfasts," *The Washington Quarterly*, vol. 5 (Spring 1982), p. 58. He describes a breakfast interview that reporters from Hearst, Knight-Ridder, the *Boston Globe*, and the Baltimore *Sun* had with Haig that the author claims was designed to make up for not being taken along on the secretary's first trip to the Middle East.

5. The best example of the demand for press seats exceeding allowable capacity was Nixon's trip to China in 1972. Martin Schram, then a reporter with *Newsday*, was denied a place by Press Secretary Ron Ziegler. David Wise, in *The Politics of Lying* (Vintage, 1973), pp. 321–22, makes a powerful case that this was done to punish the newspaper for a series on Nixon's friend Bebe Rebozo.

6. Far beyond the outer ring there are others in Washington who also have press passes and seem especially drawn to the daily White House and State Department briefings. As Larry Speakes makes an announcement, Carl Leubsdorf, bureau chief of the *Dallas Morning News*, whispers to me that the little old lady to the right of the podium is a journalist's widow, never known to have filed a story, although she goes on all the president's overseas trips and spends her time shopping. Several days later, after a Reagan press conference, another older woman appearing in what approximates a red, white, and blue Uncle Sam outfit abuses two of the press secretary's young aides for not giving her a better seat. At the White House, William Drummond of National Public Radio notes, "We have our institutional crazies. They're like your batty maiden aunt who the family understands and puts up with." But at the State Department the regular reporters do not find the situation quite so amusing; see chapter 6, pp. 70–71.

7. Thomas E. Cronin, *The State of the Presidency* (Little, Brown, 1975), pp. 188–92.

8. Wayne Pines contends that this statement is not representative of the FDA press office's view.

9. It therefore seems especially ironic that the State Department has created the daily briefing that, like the broom in *The Sorcerer's Apprentice*, no one knows how to turn off. This institution is only of recent importance; the briefings were dismissed by a thoughtful scholar writing in the early 1960s. See Bernard C. Cohen, *The Press and Foreign Policy* (Princeton University Press, 1963), pp. 176–77.

10. See *Congressional Record*, March 25, 1966, p. A1738.

11. George Urban, "A Long Conversation with Dr. Zbigniew Brzezinski," *Encounter*, vol. 56 (May 1981), pp. 14–15.

12. See "Meeting the Press: A Conversation with David Gergen and Jody Powell," *Public Opinion*, vol. 4 (December/January 1982), p. 10.

13. Lloyd N. Cutler, "The Evening News: A 'Galvanizing Force,'" *New York Times*, July 7, 1983.

14. Representative newspaper stories of this variety include Howell Raines, "Reagan's Bold Gamble: Prime-Time TV Conference and Speeches on Radio Seeking to Improve Public Image," *New York Times*, March 31, 1982; Hobart Rowen, "Imagery High on Reagan Summit Agenda," *Washington Post*, May 30, 1982; and Robert S. Greenberger, "How Donovan Rises from Political Grave with Help of Hype: Labor Secretary and PR Staff Turn Tide on AFL-CIO, which Tried to Ignore Him," *Wall Street Journal*, June 16, 1983.

15. Survey taken by Bruce M. Brown of the FDA Public Affairs Office, February 4, 1981.

16. Lou Cannon, *Reporting: An Inside View* (California Journal Press, 1977), p. 196.

Chapter 9. Reflections on Government/Press Relations

1. "Self-respecting reporters rarely consult the PR men," claims Stewart Alsop in *The Center* (Popular Library, 1968), p. 162.
2. Carlton E. Spitzer, "Informing the People," *The Bureaucrat* (Winter 1981–82), p. 62.
3. Harry F. Rosenthal, "U.S. Devotes Millions to PR, Experts," *Washington Post*, May 30, 1983. Rosenthal concludes that 120 government agencies collectively budgeted $165 million on public information for the fiscal year, but that "the real cost is far greater."
4. For a compilation of the many ways that government public relations have been defined, I am indebted to Mordecai Kamesar Lee, "Congressional Oversight of Federal Public Relations," (Ph.D. dissertation, Syracuse University, 1975).
5. The considerable controversy in 1971 over a CBS documentary, "The Selling of the Pentagon," was not about press offices but about "staging elaborate war games, circulating propaganda films and sending out officers in uniform to warn about the menace of communism," according to Lester A. Sobel, ed., *Media Controversies* (Facts on File, 1981), p. 31.
6. As I stated at the outset, I did not set out to go to places that are supposed to be models of inefficiency. See "Author's Note."
7. See Charles S. Steinberg, *The Information Establishment* (Hastings House, 1980), pp. 151, 163.
8. Ibid., p. 54.
9. Meg Greenfield, "The Gabby American Way," *Washington Post*, February 17, 1982.
10. The following sentence from a newspaper story is as useful as it is unusual: "Information that withdrawal was under serious consideration was first made available by opponents of an American pullout who are hoping to stop it by bringing the matter into public discussion." See E. J. Dionne Jr., "U.S. Weighs Unesco Pullout Over Budget and Policy Fight," *New York Times*, December 15, 1983.
11. See David Manning White, "The 'Gatekeeper': A Case Study in the Selection of News," *Journalism Quarterly*, vol. 27 (Fall 1950), pp. 383–90; and Maxwell McCombs and Donald Shaw, "The Agenda-Setting Function of Mass Media," *Public Opinion Quarterly*, vol. 36 (Summer 1972), pp. 176–87.
12. Speaking at the same conference, for example, presidential counselor Edwin Meese said that the press plays a large part in shaping American foreign policy because of its influence on public opinion, while Jeff Greenfield of CBS News said that reporters do not have any real influence on forming public opinion or policy. See "Influence of Media Over American Foreign Policy Discussed," *More Facs* (published by the Foundation for American Communications) (April/May 1982), p. 1.
13. The questioner is Hodding Carter on a segment of the PBS television series "Inside Story" called "Mr. President . . . Mr. President . . . ?" Transcript (The Press and the Public Project, Inc., 1981), p. 2.
14. Francis E. Rourke, *Secrecy and Publicity: Dilemmas of Democracy* (Johns Hopkins University Press, 1961), p. 203.
15. For another view, see Sissela Bok, *Lying: Moral Choice in Public and Private Life* (Vintage, 1979), p. 191. Bok would countenance lying for the public good by officials if what constituted that category of lies could be "openly debated and consented to in advance."
16. A National Opinion Research Center poll shows that 13.7 percent of respondents have a great deal of confidence in the press, 13.4 percent in federal government executives, 12.7

percent in television, and 10.2 percent in Congress. See "Journalism Under Fire," *Time* (December 12, 1983), p. 79.

17. See David L. Altheide and John M. Johnson, *Bureaucratic Propaganda* (Allyn and Bacon, 1980), p. 10.

18. See Phillip Knightley, *The First Casualty* (Andre Deutsch, 1975). Also, for an account of how the authorities "frequently used the media as an instrument with which to confuse the enemy" during Britain's war with Argentina in 1982, see Robert Harris, *Gotcha! The Media, the Government and the Falklands Crisis* (Faber and Faber, 1983).

19. Dom Bonafede, "The Washington Press—Competing For Power with the Federal Government," *National Journal* (April 17, 1982), p. 666.

20. I. F. Stone, "Many Thank-yous, Mr. President," *Washington Post Book World*, February 13, 1966.

21. Arthur M. Okun, *Equality and Efficiency: The Big Tradeoff* (Brookings Institution, 1975), chap. 1, "Rights and Dollars," is especially pertinent if the discussion were to be applied to the rationales for government press offices. Of similar value is Robert A. Dahl and Edward R. Tufte, *Size and Democracy* (Stanford University Press, 1973). Dahl and Tufte warn against romanticizing "the idea that democracy is somehow linked with smallness" (p. 12) by concluding that "no single type or size of unit is optimal for achieving the twin goals of citizen effectiveness and system capacity" (p. 138).

22. Mark Watson, a legendary Pentagon reporter for the Baltimore *Sun*, once "politely interrupted a Defense Secretary who was talking about tank production rates and suggested that the subject was a military secret, not to be discussed in public." See Robert B. Sims, *The Pentagon Reporters* (National Defense University Press, 1983), pp. 24–25.

23. Tom Hamburger, "How the White House Cons the Press," *Washington Monthly* (January 1982), p. 24.

Index

ABC. *See* American Broadcasting Co.
Aberbach, Joel D., 145n
Adams, Tom, 56
Aerospace Daily, 114
Agency for International Development, 32
Air Florida crash, *1982*, 54–56
Allen, Richard, 79–80, 81
Allin, Lyndon (Mort), 22
Alsop, Stewart, 77, 149n, 152n
Altheide, David L., 153n
American Civil Liberties Union, 3
American Broadcasting Co. (ABC), 43, 51, 52, 83, 89, 96, 99, 103, 144n
Anchorage Daily News, 44
Anderson, Jack, 80, 149n–150n
Anderson, Jim, 65, 73, 149n
Anderson, William J., 150n
Andrawis, Adib, 70
Arkansas Gazette, 114
Arms Control and Disarmament Agency, news clips, 43, 64
Associated Press (AP), 64, 65, 99, 102
Atlantic, 81–82, 144n

Baker, Howard, 76
Baker, James, 39, 80
Baker, Russell, 67, 148n
Baltimore *Sun*, 14, 43, 45, 61, 62, 63, 144n, 151n
Barber, James David, 142n
Barrett, Laurence, 149n
Barringer, Felicity, 48
Beecher, John C., 96–97
Beecher, William, 21, 25, 144n
Biggs, Jeff, 72
Bishop, Maurice, 56
Blank, Tom, 52
Bok, Sissela, 144n, 152n
Bonafede, Dom, 4, 112, 141n, 153n
Bond, David, 114

Boorstin, Daniel J., 140n
Boston Globe, 21, 144n, 151n
Bowman, William W., 145n
Brady, James, 8
Briefings, 21; agency differences in, 67–68; choice of story for, 50–51; large-scale staged, 48–49; news conference versus, 148n; participants, 151n; predicted questions for, 35; purpose, 49–50, 61; television and, 50, 71
Briefings, State Department, 49, 61, 151n; debriefing following, 71–72; guidance statements for, 61, 62–63, 69, 74, 109; participants, 69–70, 148n; questioning at, 68; room for, 64–65; television at, 65–66
Brinkley, David, 59, 83
British Broadcasting Corp. (BBC), 4
Broder, David S., 76, 149n
Brown, Bruce M., 151n
Brown, David H., 28
Brown, Harold, 18
Brzezinski, Zbigniew, 18, 144n; press relations, 104
Buchanan, Patrick, 144n
Buckley, William F., 44
Burby, Jack, 144n
Burgess, John, 147n
Burkhardt, Robert, 146n
Burnham, David, 148n
Bush, George, 40

Cable News Network (CNN), 100, 103
Califano, Joseph, 14
Cannon, Lou, 94, 106, 142n, 151n
Carlucci, Frank, 39, 87
Carter, Hodding, III, 11, 19, 20, 144n, 152n
Carter, Jimmy, 9
Casey, William, 101
Cater, Douglass, 150n
Cattani, Richard, 33

Catto, Henry E., Jr., 11, 19, 64, 142n, 147n; on Defense Department press operations, 7–8; on news leaks, 88
Catton, Bruce, 92
Causey, Mike, 42
CBS. *See* Columbia Broadcasting System
Central America, news leaks on U.S. military intentions toward, 82–83, 84–85
Central Intelligence Agency (CIA), 50, 84, 101, 150n
Chancellor, John, 59, 144n
Chapman, John Jay, 2
Chapman, William, 149n
Cheney, Richard, 72
Chicago Tribune, 81, 100, 144n
Christian, George, 22, 27, 141n
Christian Science Monitor, 33, 61, 62, 105, 150n
CIA. *See* Central Intelligence Agency
Clapp, Priscilla, 149n
Clark, William, 79, 90, 91
Clifford, Clark, 141n
Clymer, Adam, 149n
CNN. *See* Cable News Network
Coast Guard, press office, 14
Coburn, Casey, 144n
Cody, Edward, 148n
Cohen, Bernard C., 151n
Columbia Broadcasting System (CBS), 4, 5, 43, 51, 52, 57, 60, 75, 79, 99, 103
Committee on Public Information, 1
Cooley, Denton, 29
Cooney, David M., 148n
Corddry, Charles, 45
Cornwell, Elmer E., Jr., 142n
Cowan, Edward, 85
Cox newspapers, 105
Cozzens, James Gould, 143n
Crandall, Robert W., 146n
Cronkite, Walter, 104
Crises, 14; by accident versus design, 60; Air Florida crash, 1982, 54–56; Grenada invasion, 1983, 56–60
Cronin, Thomas E., 102, 151n
Cron, Ted, 55
Crossette, Barbara, 115
Cutler, Lloyd N., 105, 151n

Dahl, Robert A., 153n
Dallas Morning News, 151n
Deaver, Michael, 39

Defense Department: briefings, 61, 64, 66–67, 72; management of news, 110; meetings to disseminate information, 39, 40; news clips, 41, 44, 45, 83, 146n; news leaks in, 87–88; press office organization during crises, 14–15; press office–reporter relations, 113, 114; press officers, 7–8, 16, 32, 108, 145n; press releases, 45, 46, 47; press strategy, 103, 104–05
DeLauer, Richard D., 87
Diamond, Edwin, 142n
Diederick, Bernard, 148n
Dionne, E. J., Jr., 152n
Donaldson, Sam, 110–11
DOT. *See* Transportation Department
Drake, Bruce, 110
Drummond, William, 144n, 151n
Duchin, Ronald A., 97
Dulles, John Foster, 103
Dunn, Delmer D., 142n
Dunsmore, Barrie, 90

Education, press officers, 30–31
Epstein, Edward Jay, 140n
Evans, Rowland, 85, 86, 150n
Ezrol, Stanley, 70

Falkland Islands crisis, 49, 51, 110
Fallows, James, 144n
Farrell, Robert H., 145n
FBI. *See* Federal Bureau of Investigation
FDA. *See* Food and Drug Administration
Feaver, Douglas B., 111, 143n
Federal Aviation Administration: briefings, 49; press relations, 48
Federal Bureau of Investigation, 83, 145n
Federal government: agency responsiveness to media, 102–06; expenditures on information functions, 3; growth of activities, 2, 140n; relationship between press and, 3–4, 5. *See also under individual agencies*
Federal Highway Administration, news clips, 41
Fialka, John J., 141n
Finn, Chester E., Jr., 150n
Fischer, Dean, 12, 21, 61, 63, 71, 140n, 144n
Food and Drug Administration (FDA): assignments for press officers, 16; briefings, 48–49, 61; management of news, 110; meetings

to disseminate information, 39; news clips, 41, 44; press officers, 3, 12, 32, 34–35, 37; Public Affairs office, 9; press releases, 47–48; press strategy, 103, 106; response to reporters' inquiries, 51–52
Ford, Gerald R., 24
Fowler, John, 55
Freedom of Information Act, 143n
Freeman, James, 16
Fried, Edward R., 140n
Friedenberg, Walter, 111
Friedheim, Jerry W., 26, 64, 144n, 148n
Friendly, Alfred, Jr., 144n
Fritz, Sara J., 147n
Fulbright, J. William, 141n

Gannett newspapers, 100
Gans, Herbert J., 140n
Garreau, Joel, 150n
Gelb, Leslie, 67, 79, 83, 144n, 149n
General Accounting Office, 87, 88
Gergen, David, 8, 21, 22, 55, 80, 81, 86, 90, 147n
Getler, Michael, 150n
Geyelin, Philip, 20, 144n, 150n
Geyer, Georgie Anne, 85, 91, 150n
Gillespie, Jake, 63
Gitter, A. George, 144n
Glass, Andrew, 105
Gosden, Linda, 60, 99; and Air Florida crisis, 54–56; response to reporters' inquiries, 52–53
Goshko, John M., 68–69, 76
Goulding, Phil G., 141n
Gould, Jack, 141n
Graber, Doris A., 142n
Graff, Henry F., 145n
Graham, Katharine, 92, 150n
Granum, Rex, 144n
Gray, Richard G., 151n
Great Britain, reporter relations with civil servants, 146n
Greenberger, Robert S., 151n
Greene, Jim, 48
Greenfield, James, 144n
Greenfield, Jeff, 152n
Greenfield, Meg, 109, 152n
Greider, William, 81–82, 149n
Grenada invasion, 1983, 56–60, 113, 147n, 148n
Grossman, Michael Baruch, 140n

Gross, Richard, 45
Grunwald, Henry, 59, 99, 148n
Guidance statements for State Department briefings, 61, 62–63, 69, 109
Gutman, Roy, 143n
Gwertzman, Bernard, 66, 80

Habib, Philip, 79
Hagerty, James, 20, 22, 27
Haig, Alexander M., 9, 21, 49, 61, 146n; news leaks involving, 78, 79–81; press relations, 104
Halberstam, David, 150n
Halloran, Richard, 45, 114, 147n
Halperin, Morton H., 149n
Hamburger, Tom, 153n
Harris, Patricia, 14
Harris, Robert, 153n
Hart, Bill, 44
Hayes, Arthur Hull, Jr., 100–01
Health, Education, and Welfare Department (HEW), 37
Hearst newspapers, 4, 151n
Heclo, Hugh, 78, 141n, 149n
Heller, James, 88
Helm, Lewis M., 142n
Helms, J. Lynn, 48, 55
Hess, Stephen, 140n, 142n, 145n, 149n, 150n, 151n
HEW. See Health, Education, and Welfare Department
Hiebert, Ray Eldon, 142n
Hinds, Michael deCourcy, 149n
Hoffman, Fred, 18, 65
Hofstetter, C. Richard, 142n
Holdridge, John, 89
Hoover, Herbert, 1
Horowitz, Donald L., 143n
Hull, Cordell, 143n

Interviews: accessibility of officials for, 98–99; consolidation into press conferences, 112–13
Irwin, Don, 97

Janka, Les, 58
Jaroslovsky, Rich, 147n
Jenkins, Ray, 144n
Jerusalem Post, 39
Johnson, Haynes, 148n
Johnson, Hiram, 112

Johnson, John M., 153n
Johnson, Lyndon B., 9, 27, 66
Johnston, Oswald, 43
Johnstone, John W. C., 145n
Journal of Commerce, 14, 48, 49
Journalists. *See* Reporters
Juergens, George, 1, 140n

Kaiser, Robert G., 142n
Kalb, Marvin, 66, 110
Kanter, Arnold, 149n
Kaplan, Milton, 140n
Kaufman, Herbert, 27, 140n, 144n
Kennedy, William V., 150n
Kern, Montague, 151n
Kessel, John H., 145n
King, Susan, 96
Kissinger, Henry A., 9, 43, 65, 97, 104
Kital, Shalom, 70
Klein, Herbert G., 8, 141n, 144n
Klotz, Herbert W., 145n
Knightley, Phillip, 112, 153n
Knight-Ridder newspapers, 82, 151n
Kraft, Joseph, 79, 81, 84
Kumar, Martha Joynt, 140n
Kurtz, Howard, 143n

Laird, Melvin L., 64
Landau, Jack, 90
LaRoche, Lyndon H., 70
Lave, Lester B., 146n
Lawrence, Bill, 141n
Leaks, news, 141n; from congressional sources, 76, 149n; defined, 75; occurrence, 92; personality conflicts and, 109; reporter's skill and, 76–77; results, 92–94; types, 78–79
Lebow, Morton, 27
Lee, Mordecai Kamesar, 152n
Lester, Marilyn, 147n
Leubsdorf, Carl, 151n
Levering, Patricia W., 151n
Levering, Ralph B., 151n
Lewis, Drew, 14, 46, 52, 53, 54–55, 60; accessibility for interviews, 98–99; and Air Florida crisis, 54–55
Lewis, Flora, 85, 150n
Lewis, George, 97
Libya: news leak relating to Reagan and, 83–84; press conference on aircraft attack by, 14–15
Linsky, Martin, 142n

Lobe, James, 65
Los Angeles Times, 43, 97, 105, 144n
Lying: 111; in case of Grenada invasion, 58, 147n; by press secretaries, 24–25

McCardle, Dorothy, 142n
McCartney, James, 82–83
McCarty, Sandra, 61
McCloskey, Robert J., 60, 78, 143n, 148n, 149n
McClure, Robert D., 142n
McCombs, Maxwell, 152n
McLearn, Donald C., 146n
Martin, L. John, 146n
Mathews, David, 14
Means, Marianne, 4, 29, 141n
Media: agency strategies relating to, 101–06; government servicing of, 1–2; growing complexity of, 2; organization status, 99–100
Meese, Edwin, 39, 40, 53, 55, 79, 152n
Merrill, Richard A., 146n
Miami Herald, 72, 148n
Michel, Robert, 76
Miller, Loye, 111
Miller, Sandy, 20
Minor, Dale, 141n
Mitchell, Andrea, 109
Mollenhoff, Clark, 144n
Molotch, Harvey, 147n
Moore, Jonathan, 142n
Morgan, David, 142n
Morris, Edmund, 140n
Morrow, E. Frederic, 143n
Motley, Langhorne A., 75
Moyers, Bill, 4–5, 24–25, 27
Murray, John E., 148n
Murrow, Edward R., 4
Muskie, Edmund, 9

Nashville *Tennessean*, 144n
National Broadcasting Co. (NBC), 43, 51, 52, 66, 81, 85, 99, 103
National Journal, 4, 12
National Public Radio (NPR), 52, 144n, 151n
National security, news leaks, 91–92
National Security Council, 63, 84
National Transportation Safety Board, 54, 55
Naver, Michael R., 142n
Nelson, Jack, 147n
Nelson, Lars-Erik, 83, 149n
Nessen, Ronald, 24, 141n

Neustadt, Richard E., 92, 142n, 150n
Newhouse, John, 144n
Newsday, 143n, 144n, 148n, 151n
News release. *See* Press release
Newsweek, 21, 83, 99
New York Daily News, 82, 83, 110, 148n
New Yorker, 144n
New York Times, 5, 21, 22, 35, 42–43, 44,
   45, 49, 52, 61, 62, 64, 80, 83, 84, 92, 99,
   100, 103, 144n, 146n
Nida, Edward, 37
Nimmo, Dan D., 142n, 146n
Nixon, Richard M., 8, 9, 10
Nofziger, Lyn, 82, 149n
Nokes, Greg, 99
Novak, Robert, 85, 86, 150n
NPR. *See* National Public Radio
Nuance journalism, 68, 69

Oberdorfer, Don, 5, 80, 84, 89, 92, 149n
Ogilvy-Webb, Marjorie, 145n
Okun, Arthur, 113, 153n
O'Leary, Jeremiah, 90, 91, 105, 150n
Orren, Gary R., 3

Patterson, Thomas E., 142n
Peterson, Faye, 51
Philadelphia Inquirer, 43, 49, 82
Pierpont, Robert, 67–68, 75
Pines, Wayne, 19, 47, 143n, 151n
Pittsburgh Post-Gazette, 144n
Plante, Bill, 58
Polakoff, Joseph, 69
Pollard, James E., 142n
Powell, Jody, 22, 27, 94, 141n, 150n; on lying,
   24, 25; and news leaks, 94, 111; White
   House press strategy, 105
Powledge, Fred, 141n
Press officers: as administrators, 10–11; and
   bureaucracy, 35–37; criticism of, 4, 107–
   08; education, 30–31; hours worked, 31–
   32; and management of news, 108; methods
   for obtaining information, 38–40; prefer-
   ence for Washington reporters, 95–96; and
   press secretaries, 28–29; reaction to assignments, 16; and reporters, 29–30, 33, 35–
   36, 97–101; responsiveness, 33, 97; skills,
   34–35; staff functions, 8–9; subunit, 13–
   14; and supervisors, 12–13; titles, 9–10
Press offices: agency differences in, 17; centralization of agency, 11–12; defined, 5;

functions, 7; media strategies, 101–06; organizational methods, 14–16; rationale for
   existence, 112–13, 114–15. *See also* Crises;
   Routine activities, press office; *and under
   individual government agencies*
Press releases: agency motives behind, 48;
   contents, 46–47, 48; number produced, 45–
   46; reporter reaction to, 47, 48, 146–47n
Press secretaries: access to, 18, 33; and agency
   heads, 18–19; and career personnel, 28–29;
   choice of, 19; conduct rules, 23–26; improvement on job, 20; lying, 24, 25, 58;
   personality, 19–20, 21; political functions,
   23, 28–29; and reporters, 10, 21–22; role
   in agency decisionmaking, 26–28, 58; White
   House, 1, 4, 8, 20, 22, 24
Price, William, 1

Qaddafi, Muammar el, 83–84

Rabin, Kenneth, 142n
Rados, Bill, 37
Raines, Howell, 86, 149n, 150n, 151n
Rather, Dan, 60
Reagan, Ronald, 48, 50, 51, 56, 57, 59; on
   disclosure of classified information, 90, 149n;
   and news leaks, 76, 79–87, 91, 93
Rebozo, Bebe, 151n
Reedy, George E., 27, 75, 141n, 144n, 149n
Regan, Donald, 85
Reinhold, Robert, 146n
Reporters: access to agency heads, 98–99;
   agency relations with, 102–06, 113; and
   bureaucracy, 35–37; factors affecting status
   of, 97–101, 114, 151n; impersonation of,
   147n; management of news, 109–10; and
   news leaks, 76–77; press office response to,
   51–53; and press officers, 29–30, 33, 35–
   36; and press releases, 47, 48, 146–47n;
   and press secretaries, 21–22, 144n; reaction
   to Grenada invasion, 59; Washington-based,
   95–96
Reston, James, 59, 76, 104, 112, 143n, 145n,
   148n, 149n
Reston, Thomas, 45, 66
Reuters, 62, 64, 99, 102
Revson Project, 142n
Rivers, William L., 141n
Rivlin, Alice M., 140n
Robinson, Michael J., 142n
Rockman, Bert A., 145n

Rogers, William, 9
Romano, Lois, 24, 144n
Romberg, Alan, 35, 61, 63, 72, 90
Roosevelt, Franklin D., 2
Roosevelt, Theodore, 1, 2
Rosenblatt, Roger, 3, 141n
Rosenthal, Harry F., 152n
Rosenthal, Jack, 144n
Ross, Chris, 62
Ross, Thomas, 11, 18
Rosten, Leo C., 2, 140n
Rothschild, Louis, 36
Rourke, Francis E., 111, 152n
Roussel, Peter, 22
Routine activities, press office, 14; briefings, 48–51; information gathering and dissemination, 38–40; for maintenance, 53; preparation and circulation of news clips, 41–45; press releases, 45–48; response to reporters' inquiries, 51–53
Rowen, Carl, 144n
Rowen, Hobart, 151n
Royster, Vermont, 59, 148n
Rubin, Richard L., 140n
Rusk, Dean, 104; on news leaks, 76–77
Russell, Bea, example of guidance statement, 62

Safire, William, 43, 78, 81, 84, 146n, 149n, 150n
St. Louis Post-Dispatch, 52
Salinger, Pierre, 24, 58, 141n, 144n, 147n
Sanders, Keith R., 146n
San Diego Union, 144n
Scali, John, 144n
Schechter, Jerrold, 18, 144n
Schieffer, Bob, 79, 81
Schlesinger, James, 25
Schoenfeld, Dick, 55
Schorr, Daniel, 141n, 148n
Schram, Martin, 80, 149n, 151n
Schudson, Michael, 59, 145n, 148n
Schultze, Charles L., 140n
Seaga, Edward, 56, 147n
Seib, Gerald F., 147n
Seigenthaler, John, 144n
Semerad, Kate, 32, 145n
Shanahan, Eileen, 22, 23, 144n
Shapiro, Walter, 144n
Shaw, Donald, 152n
Sheehan, Margaret A., 142n

Shultz, George, 9, 26, 56, 57
Sigal, Leon V., 5, 42, 142n, 144n
Silverberg, David, 143n
Sims, Robert B., 58, 145n, 153n
Sinclair, Ward, 141n
Slawski, Edward J., 145n
Small, William J., 4, 141n
Smith, Don, 142n
Smith, Hedrick, 83, 99
Smith, Jack, 89
Sobel, Lester A., 152n
Speakes, Larry, 8, 19, 22, 39–40, 51, 86, 109; briefings, 21; and Grenada invasion, 58
Spitzer, Carlton E., 107, 142n, 152n
Spragens, William C., 144n
State Department: management of news, 110; meetings to disseminate information, 39, 40; news clips, 45; organization during crises, 15; press office, 8, 32, 34; press releases, 46; press strategy, 103, 104, 105; public affairs office, 9, 10, 11; public affairs advisers, 3, 12; reading file for press officers, 38–39. See also Briefings, State Department
State Department Correspondents Association, 71, 90
Steinberg, Charles S., 152n
Stockman, Anita, 63
Stockman, David, 81–82
Stone, I. F., 113, 153n

Taiwan, news leak on jet sale to, 89, 90, 92
Taubman, Philip, 83
Taxes, news leak on, 85–86
Taylor, Rush, 61, 63, 71, 148n
Teeters, Nancy H., 140n
Television: briefings and, 50, 65–66, 71; at State Department, 103
terHorst, Gerald, 141n
Terwoord, Carole Ann, 144n
Thatcher, Margaret, 50–51
Thomas, Helen, 65
Tillson, John C. F., 88
Time, 21, 59, 99, 144n, 148n
Townsend, Claudia, 144n
Trade publications, 100–01
Transportation, Department of, 9; and Air Florida crash, 1982, 54–56; meetings to disseminate information, 40; news clips, 41, 42, 44; press officer loyalty, 13; press releases, 46; press strategy, 106; response to reporters' inquiries, 52–53

Trattner, John H., 144n
Trewhitt, Henry, 63
Tufte, Edward R., 153n
Tumulty, Joseph, 1
Tyler, Patrick E., 84, 147n

United Press International (UPI), 52, 62, 64,
    65, 73, 99, 102
Urban, George, 151n
USA Today, 148n
U.S. Information Agency, 32–33, 61, 73
U.S. News & World Report, 94, 99, 147n

Valeriani, Richard, 97–98
Vance, Cyrus, 9, 19, 65
Vietnam, government misinformation on, 25,
    112
Village Voice, 141n
Voice of America, 100

Wallach, John P., 151n
Wall Street Journal, 49, 61, 62, 91, 99, 144n
Warren, Gerald, 144n
Washington Post, 5, 21, 35, 42–43, 45, 49,
    51, 52, 59, 61, 62, 64, 76, 80, 84, 87, 92,
    94, 99, 110, 144n, 146n
Washington Star, 144n
Washington Times, 105, 144n, 148n
Watson, Mark, 153n
Weaver, Warren, Jr., 149n
Webster, William, 84

Weinberger, Caspar W., 14, 57, 59, 81, 87,
    88
Weisman, Steven R., 85–86, 140n, 150n
Welles, Benjamin, 64, 90
White, David Manning, 152n
White, Graham V., 142n
White House: briefings, 49–50, 61, 63–64,
    67, 72–73, 148n; management of news,
    110–11; meetings to disseminate informa-
    tion, 39–40; news clips, 41, 44; press re-
    leases, 46; press secretaries, 1, 4, 8, 20, 22,
    24; press strategy, 102, 105, 106; rearranged
    press office, 8, 142n
White House Communications Agency, 42
White, William S., 149n
Wicker, Tom, 44, 76, 149n
Wilhoit, G. Cleveland, 151n
Williams-Thompson, Richard, 146n
Wilson, George C., 87, 88, 90, 91
Wilson, Woodrow, 1
Wise, David, 141n, 151n
Woodruff, Judy, 110
Woodward, Bob, 78

Young, Helen, 44
Young, Roger S., 145n

Zeidenstein, Harvey G., 150n
Ziegler, Ron, 10, 26, 151n
Zubkoff, Harry, 44